JACK C

CW00405760

Jack Clemo was born in 1
wall. The only son of working class par...
school at an early age. Increasingly cut off by the onset
of deafness, and later blindness, Clemo's innate poetic
genius developed under the pressure of isolation. His
certainty in the integrity of his work was rewarded
when he won the Atlantic Prize for his first novel,
Wilding Graft. This success was swiftly followed by
Confession of a Rebel, his first volume of autobiography;
the second volume, *The Marriage of a Rebel*, appeared
thirty one years later, after his marriage at the age of
fifty two to Ruth Peaty. The intervening years saw
financial hardship and the disappointment of rejected
manuscripts, but his poetry was published widely, as
was his statement of faith, *The Invading Gospel*. A semi-
autobiographical novel written in the early years, *The
Shadowed Bed* was recently published for the first time.

Alan Bold of *The Scotsman* has written, 'Clemo re-
gards himself as an ordinary man, with a dislike of
artiness; he is, in fact, an extraordinary poet.' J.C.
Trewin of *The Birmingham Post* describes the author as
'one of the most remarkable living Cornishmen . . . For
all the tumult of his life and work, Jack Clemo is a
curiously serene figure now . . . he remains an extraordinary original.' Tim Lenton of *The Church of England
Newspaper* writes, 'His faith is a shining response to
what an outside would judge to be long years of suffering.'

Jack Clemo lives with his wife in Weymouth, Dorset.
'There is a truer revelation of God in the least happiness,' he writes, 'than in years of misery.'

SPIRE

SPIRE

Jack Clemo

THE MARRIAGE OF A REBEL

Spire is an imprint of Hodder & Stoughton *Publishers*

British Library Cataloguing in Publication Data

Clemo, Jack, *1916–*
The marriage of a rebel.
I. Title
823′.914

ISBN 0 340 48895 6

*Reproduced from the original setting by arrangement
with Victor Gollancz Ltd.*

*Printed in Great Britain for Hodder and Stoughton Limited, Mill Road, Dunton Green,
Sevenoaks, Kent by Richard Clay Limited, Bungay, Suffolk.*

Hodder and Stoughton Editorial Office: 47 Bedford Square, London WC1B 3DP.

"The only hope, or else despair,
  Lies in the choice of pyre or pyre—
  To be redeemed from fire by fire."

T. S. ELIOT "Little Gidding"

"I see my way as birds their trackless way. . . .
  In some time—His good time—I shall arrive:
  He guides me and the bird. In His good time."

ROBERT BROWNING "Paracelsus"

CONTENTS

PREFACE

So MANY PEOPLE have asked me for details about my adult life, and about the origin and "philosophy" of my poems, that despite the severe handicaps of my later years I have felt impelled to set down this interpretative sketch of my experiences and my work from 1947 to 1977. The very unromantic legend about me which was built up by the press, radio and television during my thirties and forties needs to be corrected by a frank account of my extraordinary romantic quest, revealing the unity and pattern-development of the various episodes that led up to my marriage. It is this central theme which makes my story significant amid the modern flux of radical ideas on religion and sex ethics. Any courage I may have shown under material hardship is less important than even the most naïve and immature stages of my mystical search.

In glancing here and there at the background of my childhood, I have been careful to avoid repeating events already described in *Confession of a Rebel*. The incidents chosen for illustration are those not mentioned in the earlier book.

My thanks are due in a special measure to my wife, not only because my marriage alone enables me to get the past into perspective, but also because of the practical help she has given me in preparing the manuscript.

JACK CLEMO

NOTE TO SECOND EDITION

For this new edition of *The Marriage of a Rebel* I have written a supplementary chapter which brings the personal story up to 1987. Happily, the later stages of my marriage, and the social and topographical contacts they involved, had merely confirmed my optimistic faith. The Italian touch in my riper years exactly fitted the Browning motif of my first chapter.

Weymouth
March 1988

CHAPTER ONE

ABBEY AND RETROSPECT

ON A SATURDAY afternoon in July 1947 a small, grey-haired woman stood at the tomb of Robert Browning in Westminster Abbey. Through horn-rimmed spectacles her large black eyes probed the shadowy carvings and slabs of Poets' Corner with the nervousness of a country-dweller who was paying her first visit to London. She was alone, and there was an atmosphere of solitude about her: one could not imagine her as a woman who had many friends. It was as though she had spent most of her life grappling with situations so unusual that in her attempts to understand and deal with them she had lost touch with her prosaic working-class neighbours, and with the trends and interests of her own generation. Her sallow face, which had never been softened by cosmetics, was deeply lined with suffering, and the big nose and determined jaw suggested that strength of character had developed in her at the expense of superficial charm. But there was no bitterness in her expression. As she bent forward to read the inscription on Browning's tomb her face relaxed in a sort of bewildered gratitude.

The woman was my mother, Eveline Clemo, and she had come to London to renew her contact with the evacuees who had been billeted in our Cornish home during the war. Still fresh in her mind were the scenes that contrasted so sharply with the elegance and peace of the Abbey: the haphazard sprawl of white gravel pyramids behind Goonamarris, their slopes hollowed by rain and sometimes veiled in smoke from the sullen and spindly brood of stacks that guarded the engine-houses and the low, zinc-roofed kiln-sheds. The evacuee girls

racing to a safe distance, up a lane or across fields, away from
the pit-head, when the warning bell rang before a blast.
Mother could see me among them, always close to a broadly-
built, flaxen-haired girl who held my hand and urged me
forward because I hadn't heard the bell. Had I been lost in
amorous speculations, musing on a favourite Browning passage?
. . . There would be no blasting in the clay-pits today, my
mother thought, for they were idle on Saturdays. The fair-
haired girl was now back in London, and I would have to
walk in the lanes or over the fields alone, perhaps composing
another tense and truculent poem which hurled my gritty
transcendentalism at the modern world and its literary fashions.
Within a dozen miles of me was the bland, beauty-haunted
domain of Cornwall's popular novelists. Quiller-Couch and
the du Mauriers had lived and written on the nearby coastal
fringe, depicting romantic love as prim and dignified or
lushly and glamorously aberrant. A mile from my doorstep, in
St Stephen's cemetery, a granite slab covered the ashes of my
cousin, Joseph Hocking, once a best-selling author of sentimental love stories. Some twist of fate had set me apart from
these writers, and my mother's presence in Poets' Corner was a
result of this.

Amid her confused recollections a thrill of pride was
dominant in her heart, for on her way to the Abbey she had
passed the office of the publishers who had recently accepted
my novel *Wilding Graft*. It was only because of this success that
the London visit had been possible: a few months earlier she
was still struggling desperately to make ends meet, and could
not have afforded a day-trip to Plymouth, much less a week in
London. The hardship which had begun when my father was
killed on a naval voyage in 1917 had been aggravated when,
after leaving Trethosa village school in my thirteenth year
through temporary eye trouble, I became a slovenly, drifting
misfit, a dreamy loafer who wrote verse and stories at odd
moments, but could not or would not grip the practical side
of life. My mother had sometimes urged me to get a light job
on the clayworks where my father had been employed, but

though I spent many hours in the quarries and on the gravel-tips, getting my clothes torn and muddy as I explored tunnels, drying-kilns and engine-houses while work was suspended, I could not face the daily proximity of rough, insensitive labourers who read nothing but newspapers and talked about nothing but sport and the "bloody Government". In the state to which I had been reduced by an almost pathological mysticism, I would not obey a foreman or co-operate with anyone. When my mother suggested that I should apply for a job "down Goonvean or up Slip quarry", I merely shrugged or protested vehemently against a civilised, wage-earning society which worshipped money instead of being willing to starve for the true meaning of worship. Mother knew that I was emotionally starved and upset, that the love of a loyal and understanding girl would have lifted me out of this fog of maladjustment. She was very tolerant of my defensive isolationism, even though it grieved her to know that the village people regarded me as a lazy sponger or an unemployable weakling. She bravely shouldered the burden of keeping me on her small pension during the fourteen years in which I never earned more than £5 a year by my pen. She also carried the burden of looking after her deformed and retarded sister, my Aunt Bertha, who had lived in the Goonamarris cottage before I was born, and was still there, a half-bald diabetic dwarf of fifty-five, limping stolidly about and trying to get meals for me, though my cousin, Viney, was doing most of the housework while Mother was in London.

It seemed incongruous indeed that a woman with such a grim and grinding background should enter Westminster Abbey to pay homage at the tomb of Browning, the wealthy, cultured Victorian optimist who had written cheerily about God amid the glowing luxuries of Italy. Mother had not read much of Browning herself: she had little spare time for reading, and had not even read *Wilding Graft* in manuscript. But she knew that the title and motto of my novel were taken from Browning's poems, and in the dark, damp little cottage on the Cornish hilltop she had often listened patiently while I tried to explain what his vision, especially his religious approach to sexual love, was doing for me. As she stood quietly at his grave her mind went back over the twelve years in which she had frequently seen me reading his poems and love-letters, and biographies of him. She recalled me as a glum, sickly-looking teenager, my long black hair falling untidily around my face as I leaned over the desk to underline my favourite passages or write a date or note in the margin. On winter evenings I would hold the book fairly close to my eyes in order to read it by the faint light of a paraffin lamp hanging from a beam in our kitchen. When I shut the volume I would slump in silent meditation for a long while, frowning at the black Pomeranian dog Flush on the hearth-rug or sofa. Mother knew why I had named him after Elizabeth Barrett's famous dog. From 1935 onward I had expressed my conviction that if I accepted Browning's positive faith it would link me up with a pattern of recurrence that would eventually bring me a fulfilment similar to the Wimpole Street drama. My writing, which had begun through an abortive mystical attachment to a village girl of my own age who found me repulsive, must flower from new roots, from a realistic, down-to-earth grasp of a type of love and marriage which had transcendental implications, free from puritanical taboos but healthily Christian.

In my early twenties I must have looked happier as I read the books, for my Christian faith had become clear and firm (though I never went to church), and the wounds caused by adolescent frustration were being healed by the tenderness of a young schoolgirl called Barbara who lived next door to us. I shortened her name to "Ba" in my diaries to make the record seem more like Browning's love-letters, though I knew that this friendship was only a slight foreshadowing of the real drama. As I was still virtually penniless, the real drama had to wait. By the time the war brought its gross threat to all the romantic dreamers in Britain, sweeping the Browning ideal away in a flood of mismatings, Barbara had gone to live in a neighbouring village, and the new tenants next door soon offered a billet to a London evacuee girl called Irene, who became the heroine of *Wilding Graft*. She was a plump, fair-haired girl from a Roman Catholic home in the poorer quarters of Islington, and was almost as incapable of school studies as Bernadette had been. I felt protective about her, and was stimulated by her smouldering primitive heaviness. When in 1941 she was transferred to my mother's care, a new situation arose in our cottage. I still read Browning while Irene was at school, but in the evenings the books stayed on the shelf. I sat with Irene on my knee, lines from Browning's poems running through my mind, coming alive in actual contact:

> "Your small hand is a woman in itself,
> And mine the man's bare breast she curls inside."

I was dramatising inadequate experience, making it yield mature inspiration. Sometimes Irene and I would enjoy a dance in our cramped kitchen while the gramophone played a jazz record, or, after going out for a walk in the autumn dusk and noticing that the moon was coming up over the white clay-peaks of Karslake, we would glide to and fro on the rough crazy-paved path that bordered our lawn, her head on my shoulder. This was a fresh pleasure to me: I had naturally loathed dance-halls when I was a submerged introvert, and Barbara had been too small to be my dance partner.

Irene lived in my home till she was thirteen: she was with me every day while I wrote *Wilding Graft*, though she never read a line of the book. It was not always easy for me to sort out my reactions. There was a day in July 1943 when she accompanied my mother and me to Truro, and when we entered the cathedral Irene and I moved on ahead, climbed the chancel steps and stood in front of the reredos—on the spot where, in my novel, the hero and heroine are reunited. Irene held my arm and looked intently at the carving of Christ. I was strangely and profoundly stirred: it was as if the story had come true in my own life. But I knew that it was the artist in me, not the man, who felt this sense of fitness and unity. I was a penniless misfit of twenty-seven, and during the war years I had been hard of hearing, while Irene was just one of the thousands of London evacuee children who were finding temporary refuge in Cornwall. Yet as the war neared its close there were subtle changes in our relationship. Irene showed an adolescent awareness that made her either warmer or defensive and frigid. I began to be tortured by the thought that she would soon be thrown back into the fever of post-war London. The mounting strain of fear and emotional confusion affected my health, and my hearing worsened. I could not catch her farewell remarks when she kissed me good-bye in June 1945.

I tried to maintain a correspondence with her, writing brief playful letters, and at first she replied with illiterate scrawls, telling me that she was "alright" and had been to a show with her sister, or something equally banal. But in the autumn of 1946 she stopped writing to me, though she still answered my mother's messages. I felt baulked and uneasy, and when, on the acceptance of *Wilding Graft*, I received a charming and flawless letter of congratulation from Barbara, I was surprised by a sudden and strong renewal of my old feeling for her. The contrast to Irene's rebuff gave me an impulse to strike a deeper, more intimate note in my reply. Creative writers are often romantic fools, and I would not have been the first poet or novelist to send tragic and absurd outpourings to a girl who was nearly sixteen. But fortunately—perhaps because I came from tough working-class stock—I possessed a vein of hard common sense that enabled me to see things from the standpoint of ordinary villagers as well as from the artist's world of inflated and irrational fancy. I merely thanked Barbara for her letter and promised to send her a copy of the book.

It was at this juncture that my mother was invited—not by Irene's family—to visit London. We had many discussions about the wisdom or folly of my travelling up with her so that I could see for myself how Irene had developed, thus ending the suspense. Now that I had signed a publisher's contract I needed to know who was going to inspire my next book. I had always been a subjective writer, with little power of invention.

I could not, in a cool detached way, construct a story that had no resemblance to my own life-pattern. I had to be hit by an emotional crisis that generated energy: until I got innocently but deeply involved with an inspirer I seemed to have no imagination as far as romantic writing was concerned. I could produce religious poetry and controversial prose without needing the feminine spark, but as yet I had published only one poem—"Christ in the Clay-pit"—inspired by divine love alone. My mother was baffled, but she accepted the facts, and when I suggested that any particular inspiration might be permanent she would say: "Well, if 'tis God's will it'll come to 'ee. In a life so strange as yours is, *anything* can happen." We both felt, however, that my deafness would make a London encounter with Irene more embarrassing than helpful, and at Easter 1947 the whole plan was jeopardised by an unexpected stroke of fate.

On Palm Sunday I awoke to find my right eye inflamed and painful, the sight blurred, and the left eye very weak, though still clear. The old enemy, which had half-blinded me twice during childhood, had pounced again, without warning, after being quiescent all through my twenties: only three months earlier a specialist at Truro infirmary had said there was little risk of my getting any more attacks. The local doctor advised immediate treatment, and I was taken to St Austell hospital, where I remained for ten days, having penicillin injected into my hip twice a day. I was in a private ward in the east wing of the cosy little cottage hospital, the window giving a view of the green slopes dipping to the fringe of the town, the railway viaduct in the valley, and the harsher spur of moorland rising to the clay-scarred heights of Longstone and Hensbarrow. I could still see the landscape and the blue sky, and the doctor seemed confident that the inflammation would clear up. There was no seething resentment in me: the matron told my mother that I was "a wonderful patient" because I lay calm and un-complaining for hours without ringing the bell to summon help. After all, this was Passion Week, and I was supposed to be a mystic. Beside my bed on a small table was a copy of the recently published *Penguin New Writing* containing "A Calvinist in Love"—my first successful attempt to produce my own brand of the Browning love poem:

> "Our love is full-grown Dogma's offspring,
>   Election's child,
>   Making the wild
> Heats of our blood an offering."

As I lay there alone in the silent room, I wondered what sort of training a girl would need in order to understand what I was talking about. Here was no simple and spontaneous love poetry expressing feelings that everyone knew by instinct. The speaker in this dramatic monologue was concerned with a love complicated and transformed by a doctrinal interpretation, a view of the universe which apparently depended on spiritual crisis. Would the girl need to suffer, be jilted or betrayed on the natural level so that she was forced to reach beyond it? Would she have to plunge into the "wild heats" of the reputed pagan innocence, and be disillusioned there until she was ready to see and seek marriage as an "offering" within Christian worship? I could not feel that any of the girls I had yet known were likely to touch these depths of natural disintegration and spiritual renewal. Irene's Catholicism was nominal and superficial (while she lived with us she preferred my mother's Methodism), and Barbara's parents had brought her up in the Jehovah's Witness cult, in which marriage prospects are shrivelled by the imminent horrors of Armageddon. My present weakness and pain made the fulfilment of my vision look remote indeed, especially as my daily contacts with the girls of the hospital staff produced a sense of psychological as well as physical incompetence. The brisk efficient nurse bending over my bare hip, the dark solid orderly handing me my dinner on a tray—these were images of the practical wife which I had glimpsed in Browning's realism, but the mystery of womanhood seemed so vast and complex.

One afternoon when my mother was in the ward I scribbled

a few lines to Irene, as if I needed to relieve tension. I apologised for having delayed Mother's London trip through my wretched eye trouble, and added the usual facetious nonsense of the male patient about "flirting with the nurses". Mother posted the note, but there was no reply, and when the taxi took me back to the Goonamarris cottage and the curtain was drawn across the window to protect my eyes from sun-glare, I felt much like Elizabeth Barrett in the darkened room at Wimpole Street before Browning came. Flush, now feeble in old age and half-blind, seemed dazed by my homecoming and weakly licked my hand. Everything appeared to be exhausted. The doctor had said I must attend a Truro clinic for more injections nearly every week during the summer. I could only hope that the treatment would make my eyes fairly normal again, and possibly improve my hearing. I urged Mother to go to London and try to persuade Irene to come down and spend a holiday with us later in the year. The girl's circumstances had become critical. Her father had died since the war ended, and her mother was not expected to live long. If she lost both her parents she might be willing to leave London and resume life at her old Cornish billet. Perhaps the grief and bewilderment would bring a new depth into her. . . .

My mother turned at last from Browning's tomb, stole quietly out of Poets' Corner and found her way to the door by which she had entered the Abbey. She descended the steps into the hot, crowded street, her face sharp and shadowed as she hurried towards the bus-stop where she would begin her journey back to her lodgings in Stoke Newington. She knew that by this time I had pushed into a drawer, or torn to pieces, a letter she had enclosed with a copy of C .S. Lewis' *Miracles*. The message informed me that she had been to Irene's home and had a talk with her, but was very disappointed. Irene, now a fifteen-year-old factory worker, had been "going steady" with a boy friend for eight months and did not wish to return to Cornwall. The relationship which had spurred me to write *Wilding Graft* had crumbled before it reached a point where it could be taken seriously except as testing-ground for the artist. My mother could only trust blindly in Browning's and Lewis' God of miracles, and feel thankful that at least my book was in the press to justify her faith in me.

CHAPTER TWO

FRONTIER TENSIONS

———————————

THE SLATE-ROOFED granite cottage on the crossroads above Goonamarris hamlet was a fitting birthplace for an author whose work shows a preoccupation with frontiers—the boundaries between religion and sex, mysticism and morals, creed and art, personal intuition and objective truth. I was forced to write about these subjects by spiritual and emotional stresses, often by hereditary conflicts, as my father had been pagan and my mother was pious. I might have dealt with much the same themes if I had been born surrounded by clay-pits at Stenalees, or surrounded by farms in the Coombe valley. But my awareness of borderlines was certainly strengthened by the geographical position of my home. During the early war years the cottage was still an outpost. When I looked out of the back bedroom window I could see nothing beyond our garden hedge but the grim smoke-belching stacks around Goonvean pit-head and the mountainous heaps of white rubble thrown up from Bloomdale, Goonvean and Trethosa pits. When I looked out of the front bedroom window I could see nothing but the fields of Goonamarris farm slanting steeply down to a coppice, the more wild and rugged gorge of Tregargus carrying the stream between thicker belts of woodland to the south-west, and southward the green dome of Foxhole Beacon topping a broad flank of heath.

I cannot remember at what age I was first struck by the contrast of views which resulted from my having been born on the fringe of the clay country and not in its heart, but until adolescence I simply accepted the fact that the two worlds were there. I enjoyed them both in my odd stolid way—I was never quick and exuberant in my response. Sometimes I would scramble up the rutted face of Bloomdale burrow, a long curving dump which frequently, in rainy weather, spilled over into the lane outside our garden. On the summit I would feel a strange fascination, looking down on the roof of my home from what seemed an immense height, and also, in the opposite direction, down into the huge deserted pit, noting the gaunt engine-house and kiln-sheds on its eastern side, and the big iron skip-waggon standing motionless at some point of the track that mounted 400 feet from the pit-bed to the wooden tip-frame near which I stood. The whole expanse to the horizons north, east and west was a chaotic litter of white cones, flat tapering sandbanks, industrial buildings, craters, and headstocks of china-stone quarries. A railway line threaded through the maze in a wide semi-circle, skirting one or two villages and passing under a bridge not far from Bloomdale. The stark scene did not make me shudder: nothing made me shudder except school and snakes. I always had a great liking for machinery, the hard uncompromising strength of wheels and drills.

Here at Bloomdale, on a lower ridge of the dump, was a small square engine-house, and the engine-driver there happened to be my Aunt Annie's brother-in-law, so that on the rare occasions when my cousins, Raymond and Rossiter Greenslade, came over from Trethosa to play with me, we were allowed to enter the building. We would file cautiously past the furnace and the large hot boiler just inside the door, and climb some steps to the concrete platform where Mr Greenslade, sweating and oily, sat amid roaring wheels and grating levers, watching a hand move on a dial as a wire rope that was hauling the skip-waggon up from the clay-pit slapped on a drum. The floor and corrugated-iron roof vibrated with the pounding of heavy metal, while clouds of steam poured out through a pipe under the window, isolating us within the noise and heat and whirl of wheels, rods and cylinders. It would have been hell to a Clare or a Wordsworth, but I revelled in it as much as my un-poetical cousins did. I loved the suggestion of power, of things being linked up, drawn and controlled, with the timing exactly right because someone's eye was on the dial. When I began to think deeply I saw that this was a symbol of my religious faith, or of one aspect of it, but as a boy I merely took industrial crudity for granted because my family belonged to it. My father had come home from his "cores" or shifts on the kiln with his face a mask of clay-powder, and as I loathed the school examinations that were intended to lift me above his social level, I found nothing degrading or incongruous in the material features of the clayworks.

But there was the other world, the southern panorama, softly or ruggedly natural. I sometimes ran down to the coppice to pick bluebells or blackberries, climb up into the lower forks of trees, or sit on a mossy boulder in the middle of the stream, feeling the sluggish ripples chafe around my hand. I would lapse into meditation while the birds fluttered and sang among the leaves, but my thoughts were never those of a budding rural poet. I could not feel that the lush colourful growths, or the chirpings, or the brook, had anything to teach me. They were just nice, pleasant sights or sounds: nothing religious or pantheistic came through. It was here that I was closest to Blake and Francis Thompson. For me there was indeed "no such thing as natural piety" as far as intimations from meadows, groves and streams were concerned:

> "For ah! we know not what each other says,
>   These things and I."

Mystical communion with soil and seed and gently flowing water had been impossible to me all through the years in which my senses were normally sharp. I had no passion for the earth or its "spirit of beauty", though it was not until I had been stung by feminine repulses intermittently for a decade that I wrote poems in fierce denunciation of the whole romantic approach to nature. My reactions varied, of course, with the atmosphere of different places.

A few weeks before Christmas each year I went to Tregargus

Wood for holly, accompanied by my mother in my childhood, then grimly alone during my teens, carrying a saw and wearing an old raincoat and patched trousers, for I always got my clothes torn on these expeditions. I first crossed a plank bridge over the stream near the water-wheel at Wheal Arthur, and ascended the steep heath to some fields which led to a small marsh where I often got my feet wet in jumping from one slippery stone to another to reach the steps that gave entrance to the wood. The path was very narrow along the rim of the gorge, and gloomy because of overhanging trees. I felt a savage zest in fighting my way through the thicket, knocking back furze and hazel boughs that threatened to scratch or whip my face, then leaving the track and toiling knee-deep in bracken and bramble up the slope to a holly tree. There was a healthy male satisfaction in cutting off half a dozen branches, tying them together with string and bearing the prickly load away through the jungle-like obstructions. But it was a warped and superficial thrill till 1941. In that year, and the three succeeding years, Irene went with me, and there amid the rank primitive vegetation, under the frosty winter sky, I sometimes kissed her, holding a sprig of holly above her head, pretending it was mistletoe.

But long before Irene came to Goonamarris, even before Barbara was old enough to inspire me, I had grown aware that the frontier between industrialism and nature was not fixed or peaceful. The clayworks were obviously a menace to the open countryside, aggressors in a relentless war. I saw fields, patches of downs and even cottages overrun, buried under rubble or blasted to pieces as the pits enlarged. Wooden trolleys, pushed out every weekday from the headstocks at Slip quarry—where I might have worked had I taken my mother's advice—poured tons of gravel on the biggest blackberry clumps near my home, to which I had so often hurried when Mother wanted the fruit urgently for a tart. More poignant for us, and especially for her, was the obliteration of the intimate scenes of her childhood and early married life. My grandfather's old farm at Goonvean slowly disappeared. The farmhouse, in which I was conceived— for my parents left the farm only three months before I was born—had been demolished about 1924, and apart from a barn and a few corners of outlying fields, not a trace of the farm remained by 1947. Our cottage, once the only building on the hilltop, was now half surrounded by workshops and garages which Italian prisoners-of-war had helped to construct.

I had to come to terms with these changes and decide how they were to affect me as a poet. I had used the clay-pits as the background of most of my unpublished 'prentice novels, but had not then regarded them as symbolic of anything. My pre-war verse had been abstract and didactic, without imagery or with only the traditional types, as in the oddly prophetic lines called "The True Optimism" which were printed in the *Cornish Guardian* in January 1939:

> "This meandering, mild,
>> Welcome dawn
>> Ere the year is gone
> Shall for all be lost in thunders wild.
>
> "Face the worst—invite
>> No vain hope,
>> So the horoscope
> Of earth's evil shall be read aright.
>
> "And the stars be seen,
>> Stars of God,
>> Mixing for the clod
> Fires that torture that they may make clean."

It seems surprising that during the years in which I had no physical handicaps I wrote verse that did not derive at all from what I was seeing and hearing around me every day. But when the war closed and its mood of violence and destruction persisted in my subconscious, I felt instinctively that the upheaval on my doorstep could represent a soul-battle or a cosmic tension. The clayworks could symbolise either a cruel fate crushing man's hopes and ideals, or tough truth attacking sentimental falsehood. I took the latter view, partly because the former was inconsistent with my Browningesque faith, and partly because I detested the pagan slop of nature poets. From the day in February 1945 when I wrote "Christ in the Clay-pit" the new imagery was authentic and spontaneous: every few months the vein had erupted, throwing out strange industrial-religious poems, harsh yet often exultant. Some of them expressed attitudes too extreme to be permanent. It was as if the mood induced by six years of war news and blitz pictures had got mixed up with my belief in the triumph of divine grace over human nature. I seemed to be yelling defiance at Tennyson as well as D. H. Lawrence:

> "I love to see the sand and stone I tip
>   Muzzle the grass and burst the daisy heads;
>   I watch the hard waves lapping out to still
>   The soil's rhythm for ever, and I thrill
>   With solitary song upon my lip,
>   Rejoicing as the refuse spreads:
>   'Praise God, the earth is maimed. . . .' "

Even my mother thought I was "going too far", and she must have wondered what softening influence would be needed to give me a true balance.

I had not been looking forward to my mother's return from London. She had arranged to bring our two youngest evacuees back with her and to take care of them for a year, as their mother had died. The girl was seven years old, her brother nine, and the thought of these children being in the house instead of Irene was very painful to me, though I appreciated Mother's kindness to them. On the evening of their arrival I went to Foxhole bus-stop to meet them and help with the luggage. Mother looked tired, and the children were still sad at parting from their father and other relatives. There was little attempt at conversation as we walked down the zigzag road under the lee of the Beacon, crossed the bridge over the stream and climbed the hill to Goonamarris. I carried a suitcase and found it a heavy strain in the sweltering heat.

As we drew abreast of the farm on the corner I saw that a tall slim girl of twelve or thirteen, her face deeply tanned and framed by long chestnut hair, was standing near the pillar-box. I recognised her as Brenda, a girl who lived in the hamlet. She had often been in my home during the war, playing with our evacuees. Seeing two of them now returning she strolled across and chatted with them and with my mother, then accompanied us up the lane to our cottage. Presently, while Mother was attending to the children's clothes, Brenda and I slipped out into the garden where the big fuchsia bush was trailing a mass of red flowers and butterflies and bees were darting about. I didn't say much and felt rather self-conscious because my eyes were still weak, but Brenda's dusky smile and the touch of her hand somehow relieved the pressure of irony. She had agreed to take the children to school, and this gave her an excuse for calling at our home almost daily until the holidays began. Then one Saturday afternoon when she tripped in I had to tell her that my mother and the kids had gone to Porthpean beach. I half expected Brenda to hurry back home, but she stayed with me. We went across the road to the base of Bloomdale clay-dump and sat together on a gravel bank behind a clot of nettles. The hot sunshine seemed less of a mockery. . . .

Before the end of July Brenda had inspired two poems—"The Burnt Bush" and "Intimate Landscape". Though not written immediately afterwards, they stemmed from two incidents that occurred on the same day. I had scrambled with Brenda up a ragged gully of Bloomdale dump, edging cautiously around a gorse bush near its summit. Several boys were playing on the ridge, and one of them had a box of matches. In my poem it is Brenda who fires the bush: after thirty years I am not sure of this detail, but if a boy struck the match he and his companions soon ran off, leaving me and Brenda alone amid the smoke. We crept down past the smouldering twigs to the fresher air below.

"Fresh too was my desire.
I looked upon her laughing play

27

There in the gully's winding way:
A dry cool breeze had bared her clay:
Rain fosters sap and fashions mire,
  But dry clay prompts the fire."

This poem was misinterpreted by some critics, who read unpleasant sexual implications into it. The use of erotic imagery
to describe spiritual experience is always liable to be misconstrued. In my later poems I have avoided the practice: when
a married poet uses lover-like phrases he wants to be taken
literally. What I was really saying in "The Burnt Bush" was
that "a gnarled old bush of Adam's seed" had produced
doubts about divine love because of the loneliness and frustration I had suffered since Irene left me. Brenda's tender gaiety
had burnt up this sickly growth so that I could once more
affirm God's goodness.

The other poem, "Intimate Landscape", belongs to a different category. It is one of the few poems in which I present
the natural side of romantic love in its own right, uncomplicated
by mysticism. The enigma of woman's capricious and un-
fathomable moods is the theme, and the poem sprang from a
moment of insight that came to me about an hour after the
gorse bush was burnt. When we got indoors Brenda stepped
across to the open typewriter on a small table beside my desk,
and began fingering the keys. I stood close to her, watching her
face, which was flushed and moist with perspiration, the lips
pouted as she studied the keyboard. There was something stark
and unguarded in her expression. I felt awed, in the presence
of the deep "otherness" of the opposite sex. I sensed the fire
and ice latent in this girl and in all girls, including the one I
would marry. The poem was a sort of personal dramatic
monologue, exposing the basic human need I should feel when
I was married or on the verge of marriage:

"Make clear each sign lest my male clay be hurled
  To flame when it seeks cooling, or to ice
  When lava leaps in you, hot veins entice

Under a white breast I misread,
Thinking it cold, and pass unconscious of your need.
Instruct my nerves in nuance of your smile. . . ."

This poem proves that there was nothing infantosexual or
infantile about my emotional state. I had been moved by
Francis Thompson's poems about little girls, and by books
describing Lewis Carroll's abnormal fixations, but I knew that
my condition was essentially different from theirs. Thompson
had sentimentalised about Daisy and Monica because he
despaired of marriage, feeling that "life unshared" was
"ordained" for him. Carroll had turned to little girls because
he had a neurotic fear of marriage, a horror of the biological
processes going on inside a woman. My nearest approach to
this was in "The Token", published in *Confession of a Rebel*:

"No woman again, no flesh mature,
    With the serpent-stain in its tidal lure. . . ."

This was a momentary lapse from an otherwise fairly constant
affirmation of the normal adult relationship as my destiny. The
lines were written in September 1946 when prospects were very
dark. I was thirty, still penniless and deaf; *Wilding Graft* had
been rejected by half-a-dozen publishers, and Irene had
stopped writing to me. It seemed mere blind fanaticism to go
on predicting my marriage in such circumstances, and I tried
to shield myself by professing to disdain the inaccessible
paradise. My 1947 poems revealed my faith in the Browning
pattern shining as clearly as ever.

The most poignant event of that summer was not recorded
in verse. One afternoon late in July Flush soon tired and lagged
behind when attempting to follow me as I went out to join
Brenda. She picked him up and carried him on our short walk
along the clay ridges. A few days later he seemed ill, his face
sharp and pinched. We called in a veterinary surgeon, who said
that Flush's heart was weakening with age, as he was twelve
years old. He was given an injection, but when I came down

next morning I found the stiff grey body on the sofa. I buried him in a blanket in the back garden. The grief was deepened by perplexity: his namesake had lived to share several years of the Brownings' married life, while my Flush had only witnessed what seemed to be avuncular romps, party games and pleasant rambles.

In later years when I got involved with women who faced the marriage issue, and my physical handicaps created problems in "situation morality", I realised that these immature attachments had given me some very helpful training. They would look trivial now if I had not married, but it is doubtful whether I ever could have married if the friendships with schoolgirls had not kept me emotionally receptive and made me do a lot of thinking and praying about sex ethics. I was always a rebel against convention, and these unusual relationships revealed, in actual experience, how far such "breaches of the boundary" could be consistent with Christian faith and valid as an inspiration of art. By the time I was thirty I had come to definite conclusions. I was willing to break all the rules of etiquette that had ever been invented by a stuffy and unimaginative society, but I knew that a healthy outlook, free from cynicism, futility and world-weariness, depended on obedience to the basic moral laws of the New Testament. I saw the silliness and sophistry of claiming that the artist, being "creative", is under no obligation to exercise the moral discipline that would be praiseworthy in a bank clerk or a bus-driver. The artist, like everyone else, is involved in relationships with people who trust him, and if he wilfully betrays them and wrecks their lives he is as culpable as a bank clerk who acts in the same way. Universal human values must take priority over what Eric Gill called "Art nonsense". If an artist cannot produce a masterpiece without seducing a child or corrupting another man's wife, then the world is better off without the masterpiece. The inviolate mystery of childhood and womanhood is more important than a word-pattern or paint-pattern that critics can call exquisite. Harriet Shelley's cry of despair as she drowned herself makes Shelley's exquisite lines about a love which "the heavens reject not" sound hollow in their pagan hypocrisy. Browning recognised this principle: he withdrew his early admiration of Shelley on learning that the poet had been deliberately cruel to the poor child who had trustfully married him.

CHAPTER THREE

ENTRANCES AND DEATHS

My REACTIONS WHEN *Wilding Graft* was published in March 1948 showed that I could never be contented or fulfilled as a bachelor author. If material success and the achievement of worldly ambition had ever meant anything to me, I would have been elated at the way my so-called "first novel", the strange love story of Garth and Irma, was received. Over 2,000 copies were subscribed before publication, and the book was a Book Society recommendation. American rights and Swedish translation rights were soon sold, and in July, largely through the sponsorship of Cecil Day Lewis, Birmingham University honoured the novel with a £100 Atlantic Award in Literature. There were many laudatory reviews, some of them comparing me with Hardy and T. F. Powys. But a curious sense of hollowness and dissatisfaction, of "framework which waits for a picture to frame", haunted me as I filed the good news and stuck the printed notices into my press-cuttings album. My mother understood why I was depressed, and sometimes put the thought into words by saying: "Your own Irma 'aven't come—it *do* spoil it." She realised that I was no professional novelist spinning a yarn with an eye on the current market. *Wilding Graft* had been written as an act of faith. It was, so to speak, about mystic laws that must end my celibacy: I was saying things which only my marriage could prove to be true.

The few hours of happiness I knew during those months in which I experienced my first taste of fame were the rare occasions when Brenda came up to freshen me with a touch of vivacious feminine consolation. She seemed pleased and proud when I gave her a copy of the book. I did not, of course, send one to Irene, and Barbara's response to my gift copy was not encouraging. In my letter to her I remarked that some of the characters were drawn from life and named the originals. She answered rather coolly: "I recognise the people you mention—all except Irma, and I'm afraid I don't know who she is." I could hardly tell her that Irma was Irene, and I felt that I had come to a dead end with both these girls. And indeed I had, for a few months later Barbara got engaged to a young man in the Navy, and before she was twenty she had married him and flown out to Malta, where he was stationed. My past life with its specific emotional fixations had broken up completely, but at least I was freed from suspense. I knew now that in my struggle towards marriage I had not yet contacted the one who was destined to come to me as Browning had come to Elizabeth Barrett. I had been spared the sort of prolonged torment that drove Ruskin mad. Either Barbara or Irene could so easily have become a counterpart of Rose La Touche, with whom Ruskin had fallen in love when she was a child of nine, and whom he had pursued all through her teens, begging her to marry him, until she died in her early twenties and he went insane with grief. I still held a robust faith in spite of apparent ironies, since it was clear that Ruskin's breakdown was partly due to his drifting from Calvinism to atheism. My reactions were growing more healthy, for Brenda's friendship, though in no way connected with the theme and personal fulfilment of *Wilding Graft*, was inspiring me without getting me bogged in fantastic speculations.

My publishers had asked me to write an autobiographical volume as a follow-up to my novel, and I was busy on this work when the eye trouble struck me. After resting for a few weeks I resumed writing, as my sight was clear in the left eye. But my mother's letter about Irene made me feel too sick to go on with the record of my youth. What was the point of describing a life that seemed to consist of one misfortune after another, with no happy turn at the end? It is unlikely that I would have finished *Confession of a Rebel* in 1948 without Brenda's stimulus, though I was receiving encouragement from eminent literary men. Cecil Day Lewis gave me a lot of helpful advice: his humility and kindly candour made him a very congenial correspondent, even though he was, as he put it, "one of the humanists you think so ill of". In 1947 I had let him see some of my fierce clay-pit poems, and he commented: "These poems are fine work—the poetry in them suspends my disbelief"—a phrase which I quoted nearly thirty years later in my poem "On the Burial of a Poet Laureate". A. L. Rowse also sent me enthusiastic letters, responding to the atmosphere of loneliness, the pangs of the misunderstood individualist, in my verse and in *Wilding Graft*. I presented a copy of the novel to the Dorset hermit-mystic T. F. Powys, and was moved when he replied: "I have begun *Wilding Graft* and *I know* I shall enjoy it." His work had impressed me for many years despite my rejection of his pessimism and obsession with death. He, too, had chosen the unworldly borderline, the terrible wrestle with God.

Among the letters that reached me from less famous people was one from Helena Charles, an Anglo-Catholic social worker and journalist who lived near Redruth in west Cornwall. She was to become a good and generous friend to me and my mother during the next few years, and to help me to clarify and modify my attitude to churchy religion. A cultured lady, she had met T. S. Eliot while living in London, where she had written a novel that was destroyed in the blitz. Hearing A. L. Rowse's broadcast review of *Wilding Graft* had prompted her to buy the book, and she was thrilled by the story but a little worried about the theme. Though some years my senior, she had remained unmarried after being hurt by a broken engagement in her youth. She told me that the implication of my novel seemed to be that "if you believe in God you get your girl, and if you do not you don't". (Howard Spring made the same criticism in his *Country Life* review: "One has known happily married rationalists, and saints denied the fleshly consolation they would have valued.") I explained that my ideas were not quite so naïve as that. I knew that many frustrated bachelors and spinsters had been theists, and some of them had prayed for a partner and never found one. But to pray for a certain pleasure because you want it was very different from receiving a divine "grafting", a mystical sense of *vocation* which involved painful training and identified the seeker with the sufferings of Christ. I was concerned with vocation, stressing the fact that it sometimes takes place within the realm of romantic love. I left the matter there, as I was then ignorant of Miss Charles' personal history. At a later stage I could have added that God is not obsessed with marriage, and often gives people a vocation for something else—missionary work or social work or even the cloisters. My reply appeared to satisfy her, and she did not question me again until *Confession of a Rebel* was published.

In the spring of 1948 our two young evacuees were fetched back to London by their sister. My mother felt lonely, having looked after children all through the war, and again for nearly a year following her London trip. Normal talk with me was difficult: she often had to scribble her side of the conversation on slips of paper. I had never been lively company except when there were girls frolicking around to keep me from silent brooding. Aunt Bertha was growing more frail, though she was a plucky little soul and usually cheerful. She had never been quite the same since being knocked down by a cyclist in the blackout while walking home from Trethosa chapel early in the war. She had been brought into the cottage dazed and bleeding, and towards midnight I heard her screams in the bedroom as the local doctor put stitches in her forehead. After that mishap she was more of a recluse, but not a melancholy one: her strident laugh and "Lor' massy!" still echoed through the house, and each night and morning she knelt at her bedside to perform her simple Methodist devotions. Bertha was as small as a nine-year-old girl, but my mother longed for a normal youthful atmosphere, and mentioned this to a cousin of mine who had several Plymouth children boarded out in her home. This lady advised her to apply to the Plymouth authorities, and as a result a burly woman officer arrived at our cottage in

August, accompanied by two girls, Violet and Frances Allen, who were to become my permanent foster-sisters.

I had approved of my mother's action, and even said that it might be more necessary from my standpoint than from hers. When the London children left us Brenda stopped coming to our home: my literary success went stale, and the glowing weather and earth-bounty of flowers went dead. I was restless and idle, lounging about, looking at snapshots of Brenda, Barbara and Irene, or going out for walks with my new dog—a golden Pomeranian called Spark whom Mother and I had bought at Redruth kennels a month after Flush died. I would smile as I watched him racing on ahead, his little white tail curled jauntily over his back, pausing at the mouth of every path and cart-track and sniffing at the border-scrub while he waited to see which way I would take. On learning my decision he would frisk and leap around me in ecstasy, his yelps so shrill that I could hear them. But though I was a true dog-lover and had Spark sleeping on my bed every night, I was not the sort of man who could find deep comfort in pets. In my late teens an opponent in a newspaper controversy had called me sex-obsessed and sex-poisoned, and I had reacted by thinking: "Well, if that's what I am my Christianity can deal with it." Hence the feeling of vocation or priesthood in regard to the erotic. I often felt that my rarest talent was not a talent for writing, or (as solemnly pious people had said) a talent for suffering, but a talent for the erotic, for being mystical and theological about it. I spent a lot of time trying to work out the ultimate religious meaning of the minor but vivid thrills which girls had given me. I was as sure as Browning that through faith such thrills could be linked up with "the great Word which makes all things new", that the lover could say to the beloved:

> "See and make me see, for your part,
> New depths of the divine."

A young man with this vision cannot get adequate help from

dogs, or even, as far as inspiration and fulfilment are concerned, from a devoted mother. My mother prayed earnestly that I would find a wife, not because I must "marry or burn" but because I belonged to that rarer class of men who must marry or freeze.

I knew instinctively that Violet and Frances would not prolong the phase in which I had been inspired by schoolgirls. I was too old, and had written too much about mature love, to find creative stimulus in a fresh charmer who was not of marriageable age. Violet was a shy, delicate girl of twelve, Frances a more robust and impulsive child of eleven. They were intelligent, but their emotions had been starved and cramped by the official routine of the Children's Home, following the dark, fear-ridden years in which they had lived with their parents. Like Irene, they came from a Roman Catholic background, but a very unhappy one. Mr and Mrs Allen visited us separately when they were allowed to see their offspring: the mother only came to Goonamarris once, as she died in her thirties. Her husband was more kindly—a short, vigorous, bright-eyed man, almost as deaf as I was, but chuckling and cheerful when he was with his daughters. He was grateful that they were now sheltered in a clean, orderly home, albeit a Methodist one. The girls soon responded to my mother's warm affection, and I began to care for them as individuals, though before they arrived I had merely thought that having girls in the house would enable Brenda to return. They became friends of hers very quickly, and I often went for rambles with all three of them. My writing flowed again, not so much in poetry, but I finished *Confession of a Rebel* in September, then set about reshaping the best of my pre-war novels, adding new incidents which Brenda and I had witnessed as we roamed around the clayworks. This recasting kept me busy into the early months of 1949.

My prose writing at that period showed the influence of the two authors whom I was reading with most concentration—Karl Barth and D. H. Lawrence. I hadn't read a line of Barth when I wrote *Wilding Graft*, though its theological implications could be called Barthian—the emphasis on the divine decision, the divine choice, contradicting the "goodness" of man and hurling the transcendent "No" at the intellectual honesty of disbelief. I was first drawn to Barth's rugged and explosive personality in 1946 when I read his controversial treatise against Emil Brunner in *Natural Theology*. Now in his *Epistle to the Romans* I found a massive and awe-inspiring proclamation of the truths I had glimpsed through my own experience and my solitary reading of the Bible out on the clay-peaks. After wrestling through these Barthian thunders I could see how tiny the Church Modernists were. I also felt stronger in my own position. Critics could not dismiss my religious ideas as the naïve misconceptions of a village dreamer. I might be an uneducated proletarian, but Barth was a world-famous academic giant, widely acclaimed as the most profound theological thinker since Thomas Aquinas. My critics would have to dispose of Barth and the thousands of Barthian students before they could prove me wrong.

It was in my erotic revolt against paganism that I seemed to be quite alone among my contemporaries. Unlike Lawrence, whose early environment was similar to mine, the erotic writers who emerged after the second world war had no background of simple tradition, of fervid Wesleyan chapels and damp, insanitary homes where the clothes-washing was done (as at Goonamarris during my childhood) in a sooty iron boiler hoisted above the back-kitchen grate. Such conditions have psychological effects on basic instincts: when the hunger for love awakens it gets mixed up with the hymn-singing and the soot. All this was implied in my fiction and poetry, and in some of Lawrence's, but I could find no trace of it in the writers of my own generation. My Nonconformist, working-class origins and my innate pagan streak made me reflect something akin to Lawrence's mysticism before I read him. Now in 1948 *The Rainbow* stirred my mind and intuition, prompting me to explore the twilit frontier where the higher paganism comes nearest to a rudimentary, non-ecclesiastical Christian vision. But could there be a mature Christian vision of sex, or anything else, without the Church? Barth made me face this question, and so, in its bearing on my work, his teaching was linked with Lawrence's. I had a feeling that my questioning would be answered through personal contacts—and indeed it was, though a dark shadow passed over our home before the friendships ripened.

On a Friday early in March 1949 the proofs of *Confession of a Rebel* were delivered at the cottage. Aunt Bertha took them from the postman and brought them to my desk, finding the bulky parcel almost too heavy for her shrivelled arms and hands. I was soon absorbed in proof-correcting and did not notice that Bertha seemed unusually quiet. Next day my mother told me that Bertha was ill and might rest in bed for the week-end. I was sympathetic, but went on with my proof-checking, thankful that nearly two years after the eye trouble flared up I could hunt out the misprints without needing anyone's help—without even wearing glasses. Late in the evening, however, I realised that a major domestic crisis had arisen. Mother came hurrying downstairs and went immediately to our next-door neighbour, asking him to summon a doctor at once. Bertha had apparently had a heart attack. The doctor gave her some tablets which eased her, and she slipped into a coma. When Mother awoke on Sunday morning she found that Bertha, who slept with her, was unconscious, breathing hoarsely and obviously dying. The neighbour fetched my Aunt Annie, a tall sober woman, from Trethosa, and the two sisters watched at the bedside until, just after nine o'clock, Bertha passed peacefully away.

We were all shocked and awed by this sudden death. The day became remote, strained and morbid in atmosphere: the curtains drawn over the windows, relatives crowding the small rooms, the undertakers doing their grim business. I had no wish to see a corpse, and remained downstairs with the Allen girls, who had not known Bertha long enough to feel much personal loss. She had been such an odd little creature that I scarcely felt the normal grief of a nephew, yet the sadness of her fate moved me to compassion and questioning. She had endured fifty-seven years of pitiful isolation from ordinary life because a workman was killed at Goonvean clay-pit at the end of August in 1891. Another labourer had come banging on the door of Goonvean farmhouse and panted out the ghastly news. My grandmother, Jane Polmounter, who was expecting a child in the late autumn, was so upset that she was soon in premature labour. The unfortunate baby survived, but never developed to normal size or proportions. As an adult, Bertha used to tell people with evident pride: "When I wiz born they could put me in a milk-joog."

Such births were not uncommon in past centuries, and they raise serious problems for the rational theist. I was glad that Barth had broken away from the old Calvinist interpretation of divine sovereignty. I could not accept the extreme view that all disasters are predestinated by a good but "inscrutable" Will. A deity who manipulated events in order to produce tragic freaks would be a bit too inscrutable to deserve worship. I blamed the frailty of nature, the state of anarchy into which creation had lapsed after being infected by the anti-God forces of the spiritual world. This might be a Pauline or even a medieval concept, but it had been reaffirmed by C. S. Lewis, and it was not incompatible with the positive side of Calvinism, which I accepted. I saw God working to mitigate the evils of "fallen nature". Bertha's childlike religious faith had kept her above resentment and nastiness. She sometimes plodded around the villages of Trethosa and Treviscoe with a missionary collection box, knocking at every door like a cheery, grinning little gnome.

For three days after her death I struggled with the long sheets of galley proof while the coffin rested in the bedroom overhead. Neither I nor my foster-sisters attended the funeral on the Wednesday afternoon. We went to a neighbour's house in Goonamarris hamlet for tea, then climbed into a field where Brenda and some other girls were playing ball games. Even Brenda seemed strangely distant and unreal to me in the winter dusk. I stood apart, my mind picturing the farewell scene in St Stephen's churchyard. It was poignant to realise that Aunt Bertha's huge head and diminutive body would never again be borne on her tiny boots along the western lanes to her beloved chapel.

CHAPTER FOUR

A BLONDE IN THE TWILIGHT

―――――――――――

FOR SEVERAL WEEKS before my aunt died, unusual things had been happening in our cottage. I had even smuggled a manuscript out of the house, hiding it inside my buttoned coat so that my mother and Bertha should not guess that I was going to the pillar-box. A shadow which had tantalised me at intervals for two years had suddenly become substance, and I was pondering a coincidence that linked up with my Wimpole Street fixation. Browning had first written to Elizabeth Barrett in the January preceding his thirty-third birthday, and in the January preceding my thirty-third birthday I wrote to a young poetess because my gamble with the smuggled manuscript was successful. All this sounds rather mysterious, but nearly everything in my life has been mysterious. My poems and prose books could not have been produced by a man whose experience was so ordinary that it could be summed up in a neat quotation from Shakespeare. Life has always pushed me to strange borderlines where the fantastic becomes the only normal thing. In a sense, all artists live in a world of their own, struggling with problems of inspiration that average people know nothing about. These problems can be isolating and perplexing even if the artist stays morally wholesome and holds a fairly orthodox faith. The whisper of creative intuition concerning a face, a name, an aura, leads to the edge of a precipice where there may be either a miracle or the fading of a trusted gleam.

From the end of 1946 onwards I had often, when alone at my desk, taken a large newspaper cutting from a drawer and studied it intently and quizzically, as if it might be "loaded with fate". It was a long poem in which a sixteen-year-old girl called Eileen described both her Evangelical conversion and her passionate love of natural beauty. The blank verse was remarkably good for so young a writer, and the blending of the two themes was as unforced as in Browning's "Saul". That great poem might have taught me that rapturous appreciation of nature is not necessarily pagan, but I had argued that I must write in my own way, as a rough working-class poet, and not imitate the more refined aesthetic values of a middle-class Victorian. This girl's poem, however, was a challenge nearer my vulnerable point. It was printed in a working-class religious paper, and accompanied by a photograph of its plump, fair-haired author. I had to admit that the verse moved me more than the picture, which showed a cast of features that somehow didn't appeal to my male taste. I resisted an urge to write to the girl, as I was not sufficiently sure of my reactions. But early in 1949 a fervent prose testimony which she contributed to the same paper impressed me so much that I wrote an article on similar lines, thinking it might gain the editor's approval. No one in the house knew of my intentions: my mother supposed that I was typing more pages of my revised novel when in fact I was typing a bit of religious journalism through which I would decide whether or not I should tell an eighteen-year-old poetess that she had made me feel uneasy about my non-church ritual of excavators and steamy kilns. If my article was refused, this would be negative "guidance" in the best Oxford Group tradition, and I would not approach Eileen. I slipped out of the doorway almost guiltily with my hidden manuscript, and gave Spark a nice long run to Trethosa pillar-box.

Within a week I received the editor's acceptance. I concealed the letter as I had concealed the manuscript: this venture must be kept secret until I knew Eileen's response. I wrote to her as soon as I could snatch a few minutes of privacy, explaining that her article had prompted mine, and urging her to stay "as you are now, 'all a wonder and a wild desire' for the things of the spirit". I hoped she would recognise the Browning quotation.

I had no idea where she lived, and addressed my envelope to the newspaper office. The days passed while I tinkered with my novel, teased the Allen girls, and loitered around the garden at the time of mail delivery. At last, early in February, the reply came—from a missionary college in London, where Eileen was employed as a typist. Her letter was long and eager, showing her inner loneliness, the relief she felt at being able to share her two deepest levels with another literary convert. She loved my quotation and commented on the force of "wonder" and "wild": "How expressive a 'w' is—what other word than 'wind' could express that element so impressively?" She knew the intoxication of words and of all forms of beauty, but it was clear that her work in a missionary college, and her spare-time activities at a Baptist church, had made her question and distrust aesthetic thrills. Her nature seemed to be all poetry, fluid rhythm and fancy and dreamy whispers, but she was painfully submitting it to church discipline. She taught a Bible study class and had joined an evangelistic team of ordinary young people who often went to Speakers' Corner in Hyde Park to "win souls for Christ". By these mortifications of self (a Protestant counterpart of Gerard Manley Hopkins' fasts and vigils) she was trying to knock poetry, as a worldly art, into its true place.

When I finished reading her letter I was sure that here was the closest affinity I had yet reached. I bore the same inner scars, even though I had mortified the aesthete in me by tussling with St Paul's epistles amid the tarred pulleys and slag-heaps of the clayworks. I wrote a lengthy answer to Eileen, which must have shown her that this was no casual pen-friendship. In her next letter she said: "How strange that you and I should be led to correspond in this way, for I feel we have something in common which the world would not understand, and that we each have a message for the other which God knew we needed." Her "message" for me was obviously connected with the two points that I had become worried about —my vilification of nature and my rejection of churches. Such a major influence could no longer remain secret, especially as my article was published in mid-February. I explained the situation to my mother, who was surprised but very sympathetic, feeling that I was now more mature and normal, beginning an attachment with sensible discussions, a young woman taking me seriously. I could reveal to Eileen many aspects of my faith and spiritual experience which I had never disclosed to my mother, and as the winter softened into spring I revelled in an altogether new state of liberation. Eileen sent me more of her verse, some of which I thought too sentimental, about birds and butterflies. I sent her *Wilding Graft*, which she thought too harsh and bitterly Kierkegaardian in its non-church religion. We exchanged several photographs: the snapshots of me on the clayworks made her shudder, and she told me that if Cornwall was really like this I ought to leave it, for my readers' sake as well as my own. The place was making my writings ugly and inhuman, warping my picture of Christianity. An excavator tearing up flowers was *not* a true symbol of divine grace removing sin and error from the human soul. . . .

We argued and preached and teased each other, trying to clarify our aims and motives, our failures and misgivings, and our awareness of what we still needed. I spoke of my belief in a Wimpole Street vocation, and at first she seemed perplexed and hesitant about it. "Why are you so *sure*? . . . God may have quite other plans for you." I then posted to her a copy of "Intimate Landscape", which had just appeared in the *Cornish Review*, and the poem melted away her defences, leaving her starkly emotional for a moment. A man who had been given such profound understanding of a woman's heart and nerves was obviously being prepared for something more than an imaginary love. . . . I asked her frankly if she had ever thought of our relationship becoming more than a friendly contact, and she admitted that the idea of marrying me had at times hovered in her mind, but always with reserve and uncertainty, not because of my deafness but because none of the photographs I sent her had aroused a flicker of physical response in her. We both faced the same problem—an apparent total lack of

sex-appeal. I loaned her some of C. S. Lewis' books in which
he pointed out that a romantic "falling in love" is nowhere
mentioned in the New Testament as an essential preliminary to
Christian marriage. Unions based on physical passion often
ended in divorce. Couldn't Christians pioneer a different kind
of marriage, based on a complex faith which used the senses
sacramentally without a biological itch being whipped up and
glamorised? Eileen agreed that the spiritual side should come
first for Christians, but she still felt that a marriage in which
there was no rapturous enchantment of desire would be a sort
of mortification. If God demanded this she would accept it as
she had accepted the mortification of her romantic ego by
putting evangelism before poetry.

The tone of our correspondence changed after this crisis.
Sometimes our letters were entirely practical, concerned with
questions of residence, budget, our simple tastes in food, dress,
furniture: it was as if we were already planning our home.
Sometimes we were moved by a mystical glimpse of the marvel-
lous ways of Providence, and enclosed new verse with our
letters. The chief product of this mood was my poem "Priest
out of Bondage", written when we had virtually decided that
if we ever did marry we would settle outside Cornwall:

> "I take the irrevocable step beyond
> Loyalty to this dead land: no longer bone
> Of my bone is its granite, nor flesh
> Of my flesh its clay:
> The bright blade of the Word severs the barbarous bond."

But there were also distressing moments when Eileen wrote of
her sleepless nights, migraines, inability to concentrate. On a
visit to her home in a village near the Essex-Hertfordshire
border she told her parents about her dilemma, and when they
objected that I was too old, too handicapped and too poor she
begged me to write to them, which I did, but without effect.
The summer dragged on in suspense and turmoil. She suggested
that I should meet her in London, but I felt I could not do

justice to myself there, as my mother would have to come with me. If only she, Eileen, could manage a Cornish holiday. . . . But her parents planned to take her to the Norfolk Broads. We saw no way of developing our relationship. We could not write love letters until we fell in love, we could not fall in love until we met, and we were afraid to meet lest the first glance and handshake confirmed the fear of physical incompatibility. Yet in faith and temperament we were so perfectly matched that the feeling of guidance and design was always with us.

I went through various shades of reaction as I finished my novel, baffled by the complexity of inspiration, for Barbara had inspired the first draft, Brenda the second, and Eileen the final touches. I had discussed the book with her, and she was uneasy because I was still preoccupied with raw industrial realism: she wished to inspire something with more beauty and colour in it. When the manuscript had been posted to my agent I lapsed into idleness, going for walks with Frances and Spark and more rarely with Brenda, whose appeal became vivid again, though in a subtly different atmosphere, as the shock of Aunt Bertha's death wore off. I soon adjusted myself to living in the cottage without the familiar shrill "Lor' massy!" and the sight of little Bertha standing on a low stool or "cricket" in order to make herself tall enough to help Mother at the wash-tub.

During the school holidays there were brief distractions—day-trips to beaches, visits to farms owned by my relatives, and two more memorable excursions. The longest was a trip to Plymouth at the invitation of Mr Allen, who wanted Violet and Frances to see his new lodgings. My mother accompanied us on the train from St Austell, and the journey revived my recollections of those pre-war days when I had often gone to Plymouth alone for medical treatment at a clinic. Crossing Saltash bridge had always thrilled me: the sense of a frontier again, but more poignant and exotic than that at Goonamarris: there was a strange pang of elation as I glided above the moving waters, seeing the Cornish shore recede, the Devon one draw nearer, the boats looking small and vulnerable down there on the quiet tide. Now in 1949 the whole stretch of country was haunted and sharpened by the crisis about Eileen. As we were borne out of the clay district along the lush fringe of the river Fowey, and then over bridges in the densely wooded Glynn Valley and on to the flat pastures and thickets around the Lynher, I was reminded of the softly pretty landscapes of Essex and Hertfordshire which had moulded Eileen's character. In my youth I had regarded the sylvan scenes of south-east Cornwall with the same sort of mild interest as I felt in Goona-marris copse, but now they seemed to reflect something deep and relevant, tremulous with possibilities.

When the train stopped at North Road station Mr Allen was awaiting us on the platform. He looked more nimble and round-eyed than ever as he greeted his daughters and escorted us through the ticket-barrier, chattering in jovial indifference to his inability to catch what was shouted at him. We were soon on a bus, heading out of the high suburbs into a part of the city I could not recognise. The Plymouth I knew had been battered and scorched into rubble by the fire-raids of 1941. Scars of the blitz loomed jaggedly beyond the bus windows. We alighted in the working-class quarters and walked through mean streets to Mr Allen's lodgings. The house was drab in appearance, and as we climbed the long flight of stairs inside it my mind suddenly, through some trick of association, picked up a literary parallel from the past. I seemed to be ascending the musty stairs of an eighteenth-century lodging-house, mounting to a garret where a ragged, half-starved poet was trying to write an epic at a rickety table. The fancy was hardly justified: Mr Allen was neatly dressed, and his apart-ment had some decent furniture in it, though it was a bleak and cheerless place. While I stood with my mother and the girls, watching Mr Allen darting about, proudly showing us his possessions, I felt an ache of pity for the man. He must have married with high hopes, and all the bright prospects had crumbled to this. His wife was not here, and tonight his children would be asleep in my home forty miles away. I had nothing

47

to moan over in comparison with such a wretched anti-climax. . . . We did not stay long in the room. Mr Allen led us away through other streets to the home of one of the girls' aunts, where we had tea. This house was more comfortable and the people were friendly, but the contacts revived unhappy memories in Violet and Frances, and they were glad when we boarded the train that would take them back to their new life among the clay-dumps.

Our second excursion was a steamer trip down the river Fal in mid-August. My cousin, Annie, drove us by car to Truro, and when I had stepped on to the vibrating deck of the boat at Lemon Quay I looked across at the cathedral. My exultant moment there with Irene six years earlier was unreal and trivial now: I had moved into broader channels. As the steamer ploughed away downstream past the wharves and warehouses, around the bend where the river became clean and flanked by heavy belts of trees on the enclosing slopes, I could feel that I was in Eileen's world again. Yet there was shadow and tension in it; and when, a few miles further south, we passed the sullen hulk of a battleship moored near the west bank, I was conscious of a real menace, especially as the dazzle of sunlight on the water was inflaming my eyes and causing a slight blur in my view of the bristling grey shape. At Falmouth I tried to relax into a holiday mood, paddling with the Allen girls and my cousins on Gyllyngvase beach. The wide sweep of the bay with its churning vessels and brisk yachts was superb in its suggestion of freedom. I enjoyed a pleasant afternoon and was patient in the shopping centres while the ladies of the party contemplated bargains; but on the return journey the excursion schedule went wrong. When we reached Malpas, where the Fal forks eastward and the main waterway becomes the Truro river, we learnt that the tide was so low at Truro that the steamer would be unable to land us there. We had to make an emergency landing at Malpas, dropping from the steamer into a motor-boat that took us ashore. I managed the jump without mishap, and we caught a bus back to Truro.

But that day ended under a dark cloud of disappointment.

On arriving home I found inside the door a letter from my agent informing me that my publishers had refused my re-written novel on commercial grounds. The agent was still keen on it and would try to place it elsewhere, but the setback had come at an awkward moment. Eileen's family were doing their utmost to show her the folly of regarding me as anything more than a pen-friend, and the rejection of my book would strengthen their case. I could not conceal the bad news, however, and when I got Eileen's reply I found that the attack had moved to a different front. She did not seem greatly perturbed about the novel: she had a dreamer's evaluation of material ups and downs, and also a daring Christian "gamble on God" spirit. Her deep and increasing worry now was about my deafness. The commonsense arguments of her parents were making her realise the unbearable strain of living with a man with whom she could never converse normally. The embarrass-ment of introducing a deaf husband to her friends. . . . There were complaints that I was writing to her too often, not giving her a chance to examine the problems in a calm and detached way. She therefore proposed that during September we should not correspond but simply pray for my healing. If the miracle occurred, her family's objections would collapse along with her own fears of physical incompatibility. If nothing happened, we must assume that the divine purpose in linking us up was not marriage but only a new phase of illumination and adjustment.

I was surprised by this abrupt and arbitrary appeal to the supernatural, but I agreed to carry out her plan: it was clearly the product of desperation. The girl had borne her lonely struggle long enough. I had no assurance about the miracle, and when September came and Eileen's letters stopped, every-thing seemed to go dead except that *Confession of a Rebel* appeared in the bookshops. I groped through the tense days until, near the end of the month, I received Eileen's letter of refusal, with an explanation of the final stage. The constant pressure from her family had made her feel the need of counsel from some impartial person whose judgement she could trust.

While on holiday in Norfolk she had met a minister who had been connected with her church, and she told him all about her predicament. He had supported her parents' view and strongly advised her to break off her relationship with me. This verdict from a spokesman of the Church had apparently settled the matter without her having to wait a few more days to see whether the healing miracle occurred.

It was not until the following year that I realised what a drastic psychological change had taken place in me through this extraordinary friendship. For eight months I had been pouring out to a young woman my innermost thoughts and longings about God, sex, marriage, and the spreading of Christian truth through art. I could never be the same man again. From 1949 onwards it was impossible for me to express a savage glee at the destruction of earthly beauty. There could be no more poems like "The Plundered Fuchsias", in which pagan sexuality (symbolised in the fuchsia flowers) is rebuked by a child's kiss:

"She marred the rhythm of earth,
    She checked fertility,
And then, the last flower trampled on,
    She turned more naughtily
    And gave her lips to me."

The soft sway of a young feminine personality, which shared my faith but was free from my distortions, had begun to clear away the effects of deep emotional wounding. Of all the people I then knew, she was the only one who could have done it. My mother had always found me stubborn. I would not listen to her when she told me to go to chapel, or get a job, or "look a bit more tidy". I hadn't listened to her when she said that my readers would think me a crank if I wrote religious denunciations of flowers. My quirks had sprung from lack of a mature girl's tenderness and understanding. Eileen had given me these qualities, with the admitted possibility of our marriage, and so she had succeeded where my mother and male friends (or mere friends of either sex) must have failed.

But there was irony in the fact that this warm light was quenched just as *Confession of a Rebel* made its appearance. Most reviewers thought it a bleakly original book, but such a savagely Kierkegaardian record of raw experience could hardly attract a war-jaded public which had grown tired of explosions. C. Day Lewis and A. L. Rowse were soon sponsoring an appeal to the Royal Literary Fund, and my small earnings were augmented by a substantial grant. This was an unexpected boon, and made me feel much more secure and protected as a writer. But I knew it would be useless to tell Eileen that the financial strain had eased. Her rejection of me as a husband was final, and my inner world was often dark and desolate in the closing months of that year.

CHAPTER FIVE

DORSET PRELUDE

WHILE I WAS still in the first bewildered flux of reactions after the abrupt end of the Eileen episode, I received letters from two older women who were also to become my temporary friends, but without emotional complications. Both were known as writers, though not creative artists. One of them might have been regarded as a symbol of the dignified Church, the other of wild nature, so they were relevant to the adjustments I had to make as a poet of faith and instinct. They were Helena Charles (who had already approached me about *Wilding Graft*) and Monica Hutchings, the Somerset author of books on rural life. Miss Charles was no longer interested in marriage and Monica was already married, thus there was no risk of painful situations arising through shy hopes or dark motives being read between the lines. I was not the sort of poet who tries to force an amorous element into all his contacts with women. I had no marriage mania, and never had to check myself on the verge of indiscretions when writing to a woman who was obviously not meant to figure in my "intimate landscape".

I was not surprised that Miss Charles should write to me again soon after the publication of my autobiography, for I knew the book must raise awkward questions for an Anglo-Catholic. She told me she had read it with fascination, but was baffled by my religious attitude. "I am perplexed by your acceptance of dogma and apparent rejection of the Church, for without the Church where is the authority of the dogma?" I replied that the authority of the dogma was in the Holy

Ghost, Who could make doctrinal truth a basic power in the life of any person, inside or outside the churches. She seemed rather wistful about this, saying she admired the simplicity of my direct mystical way to God and felt that it might offer a much-needed challenge to an over-organised Establishment. She proposed to write an article on my life and work for an Anglican paper, and would like to visit Goonamarris to get background material.

One afternoon in the late autumn she stepped into our cottage. I rose to greet a tall, dark-haired lady, not fashionably dressed but with an air of refinement and a pleasant, serious face. She had a long discussion with my mother while I slumped at my desk, speaking only when queries were jotted down and handed to me. When she had gone my mother commented: "A nice woman, but she eddn jolly—she dun't never what I call laugh." What Mother called laughter was, of course, the hearty roar of a labourer's wife or the ear-splitting, cackling scream of Aunt Bertha. Miss Charles' interest in my work was confined to my prose books: she had no taste for poetry or anything musical. It was as if she had been so hurt by the break-up of her youthful romance that she avoided everything that would remind her of the soft, illusory spell. Her favourite subjects were theology and sociology, and she was also a keen supporter of the cultural side of Cornish nationalism, with which I had no patience at that time (though twenty years later, when marriage had made me more tolerant, I accepted a Gorsedd bardship myself). "He repudiates his Celticism," she wrote sadly in her article. But she was angry as well as sad when all the papers to which she sent her manuscript refused it, even those which had often published her contributions. The editors could not feel that I was the sort of writer whom Anglicans would find either valid or edifying. I was apparently some uncouth village Fundamentalist with an unpleasant erotic streak. . . . I tried to console Miss Charles, we remained good friends, and she endeavoured to help me in other ways, chiefly through the Church's ministry of healing. I did not guess then how far this would take me from both the clay-pit mud and my mother's and Eileen's radiant Non-conformity.

However isolated a writer may seem, he can never be really insulated after he has published a book. Letters from strangers bring him in touch with a variety of backgrounds, personalities and viewpoints, and if he has reached a stage where his own outlook needs to be enlarged and modified he will find his mail as helpful, or confusing, as the books he reads. After I lost Eileen's guidance I had to grope for new directions, and the influences that touched me during the next year or so were often contradictory. If I required an antidote to the grave and earnest Catholicism of Miss Charles, there could not have been a better one than that provided by Monica Hutchings, whose first letter arrived at the end of December. *Confession of a Rebel* had been among her Christmas presents, and she was delighted to read my tribute to T. F. Powys, whom she had come to know through his brother Littleton. She was soon to visit the great hermit-mystic at Mappowder, and as he already admired my work there might be a possibility of her taking me to see him later if I could travel up from Cornwall to stay at her home near Yeovil.

This startling prospect confirmed my instinctive feeling that my horizons would remain broad. My personal world could never be narrowly Cornish again. The authentic flash from the Essex-Herts border had called me

> "Out of the bitter moorlands where my tears
>   Fell on the sullen bramble and the dun
>   Rock of the derelict years."

As dusk folded in on the last day of 1949 I climbed to the top of Bloomdale clay-dump and stood looking intently eastward, like Moses on Pisgah, wondering what message or gift the Dorset of Powys and Hardy held in store for me. I had reread these novelists since their names were mentioned in reviews of *Wilding Graft*, and had found them more congenial than any Cornish writer. They were elemental and primitive seers who had spent their lives asking ultimate questions from the standpoint of simple village realism. They had been dissatisfied with all the answers, but they knew they wanted Christianity to be the true one. This baffled longing to join the "bright believing band" had produced good fruit in humility and compassion. I could not follow them spiritually, but I was close to them in their stark, unsophisticated view of the infinite pathos of the heart's attachments—a fact which Christianity has never changed.

Monica Hutchings was a very different kind of writer, and at first she feared that we had nothing in common and that I would not be interested in her or her books. A breezy extrovert, she had escaped from formal education in her early teens, worked in a Yeovil cinema, and then gratified a gipsy streak by living alone for several years in a remote, unmodernised cottage a few miles from Sherborne. Her account of these adventures in the books she gave me was vivid and entertaining, though without any mystical or philosophical penetration. She was an unusual mixture and had soon told me that she did not drink, smoke, dance or believe in God. I liked her warm-hearted, forthright letters, full of gossip about her busy life at Church Farm, the girls she was training in her village ballet class, her constant fight against blood sports, and her acquaintance with the Powys family. I was sympathetic to all these topics, and very grateful to her when a definite arrangement was made for my mother and me to come to Church Farm in the summer, have tea with Theodore Powys at Mappowder lodge, and dine with Littleton at Sherborne. Monica planned and discussed everything with hard-headed practical sense: I could not reveal to her the deeper self I had shared with Eileen. The idea of a holiday visit to Dorset having any significance in a divine plan would have seemed silly to her.

All through that winter the spiritual part of me was nourished by the sermons and religious poems of John Donne, so I had to live on two levels. A bubbly postcard or letter from Monica would plop on my desk while I was being moved to tears by reading the prayers of "The Litany":

"Re-create me, now grown ruinous:
My heart is by dejection clay,
And by self-murder red.
From this red earth, O Father, purge away
All vicious tinctures that, new-fashionéd,
    I may rise up from death before I'm dead."

The more I studied Donne's work the more sharply and thankfully I realised that he was one of the few great poets who had passed along my Via Dolorosa and spoken my language. I could not evaluate his *Divine Poems* objectively as mere examples of another poet's art or another poet's psychological state. These passionate utterances could not be dated or labelled. Donne was not reflecting medieval theology or seventeenth-century metaphysics or an English Protestant reaction against the sloppy humanism of the Renaissance. He was voicing the timeless experience of all Christians—the mystery of a conversion process. He knew that the spiritual gleam can be distorted by the carnal flicker, and that through repentance the flicker itself can become a pure flame of the senses, intensifying the illumination of faith. Marriage had taught him the same lesson as it taught Browning and Patmore—the refining power of womanhood when explored and fulfilled within transcendent grace. But he had plumbed the mystery at a more awesome and convulsed level because of his lecherous past, and this made him more desperate about human sin. At one point he was closer to me than Browning: he had a keener awareness of the discord which Eileen and I knew so well—the tension between the natural urge to create poetry and the post-conversion urge to preach and evangelise.

It may have been partly because of my profound response to Donne that my superficially enjoyable correspondence with Monica was suddenly interrupted by a major spurt of poetry-writing—the first I had experienced since Eileen dropped me. In a single week of February 1950 I produced half the poems in *The Wintry Priesthood*, and also the poignantly human poem "Shuttered", which belongs to the same class as "Intimate

Landscape" and was inspired by the same person. Brenda had come to Violet's birthday party in January, but as she was now quite a young lady, slightly taller than I, she had not encouraged the "freedom and innocence I knew before". The poem expresses the mature pang, the effect of woman's frigidity within marriage:

> "Is it a shuttered mood, apart—
> Caprice within the nerve, or passion staled?
> I can only wait, with a heart
> So vulnerable, trust still for love unveiled."

The day after penning this dramatisation of personal feeling I wrote the imagist portrait of T. F. Powys, "A Kindred Battlefield", and the switch of interest set me off on a series of objective pieces. The poems on Spurgeon, Lawrence and Barth soon followed, and a little later the Kierkegaard poem. The whole sequence, when I finally built it up with earlier and subsequent poems, presented the theme which Eileen and I had sometimes discussed—the difficulty of maintaining a Christian priesthood of sex during a winter of theological apostasy. The mystical Christian view of marriage can make a wide impact only when orthodox doctrines about the redemption of the body are widely held. Diluted theology implies naturalistic sexuality: instincts cannot be transformed by supernatural grace while people listen to Church leaders who say there is no such thing as supernatural grace. That was why I turned my back on the churches as soon as adolescence made me aware that sex needed to be transformed, that it was a mystical force with a strong anti-Christian bias (as Shelley, Swinburne and D. H. Lawrence claimed), yet potentially the point where human love fused most perfectly with the love of God. The struggle to find clues as an outsider, without the help of an understanding girl, had produced such tortured poems as "Prisoner of God", "The Child Traitor" and "Clay-land Moods". But now in my Barth poem came the first hint of a possible reconciliation with a reviving orthodox or neo-orthodox

Church. Here I admitted that corporate worship might be necessary to correct a mystical poet's subjective aberrations:

> "The bed and battleground of solitude
> Lie thawed in fellowship; my symbols fade
> In recognition of the Citadel."

It was Donne's Citadel as well as Barth's that I had in mind, and Eileen's influence was certainly there, but not, at that early stage, Miss Charles'.

I received several letters from Littleton Powys after Monica had got him interested in me, and I was deeply impressed by his accounts of Theodore's quiet and private return to the Church. It seemed that I would be meeting the hermit genius at just the right time, when his spiritual odyssey was running parallel with my own. The clash between his Evangelical up-bringing and his darkly pagan nature had made some of his writings bitter and blasphemous, but it almost ceased as he advanced into old age. He had abandoned writing over a decade ago, feeling, as Eric Gill had felt, that an artist's defiantly religious emphasis on self-expression is a sickness, a disease of the ego. Powys had found happiness in a completely idle life of simple domestic monotony and daily devotions in church. One of Littleton's letters to me recorded that on his last visit to Mappowder he had met Theodore coming out of the church with the rector: the two of them had been worshipping together in the prayers and responses of Cranmer's Litany. Theodore was reaching back to the world of Donne, though his hermit streak still prevented him from joining the Sunday congregations. I was at much the same point, not yet ready for the family pew and the collection box, but spiritually closer to the normal communion of believers. I was forty years younger than Powys, however, and did not intend my release from isolationist nightmares to be kept secret.

Monica had loaned her copy of *Confession of a Rebel* to Littleton, and my praise of Theodore was almost the only thing in the book with which he agreed. "You probably can see into his mind better than I can," he wrote, and this was not surprising, for Littleton was a kindly but conventional retired schoolmaster, voluble about the half-century he had devoted to education, sport, travel and middle-class comfort. He was a liberal Anglican in religion. I sent him one or two of my new poems, and though they were not the type he really enjoyed—he put Matthew Arnold far above Browning—he appreciated them as evidence that "an inspired art is not to be taught except by the Holy Ghost"—a statement that raises awkward questions about blasphemous art and the remorse of John Donne over the inspired art of Jack Donne. I admired Littleton's tolerance and generosity, but most of his tastes and ideas were outside my range. He seemed to think that the solution of the world's ills lay in field natural history. He had "never known two field naturalists who did not get on well together": the study of plants and beetles made men conscious of the Creator. . . . I preferred Monica Hutchings' unsentimental realism. She was then writing her autobiography, *The Walnut Tree*, in which she asserted that her passionate love of nature had never brought her the slightest intimation of a personal God.

In the early summer Monica came down to Goonamarris, discussed plans for our Dorset visit, and scrambled around the clayworks with me and the Allen girls. She was rather small but well-built, and looked very youthful in her blue slacks, her thick black hair tossing over her shoulders. She had a broad smile for everyone, and the gipsy-like slant of her dark eyes fitted the aura of rural freedom that pervaded her. Even my mother found her attractive and lost any nervousness she may have felt at the prospect of spending a few nights on a lonely farm a hundred miles from the clay-pits. In the fourth week of August we travelled to Somerset by train, taking Spark with us. Violet and Frances, being now teenagers, could manage on their own for a day or two. The journey seemed a long one, and the landscape beyond Plymouth was strange, a trifle blurred to me as the hot dusty compartment and sudden draughts irritated my eyes. But we reached Yeovil in the late afternoon, and Monica took us by car northward to Barrow and the rambling farmhouse about which she had written so much. Spark slept in my bedroom that night, and next morning Monica led us through the big fields, explained the topography to my mother, and scribbled some notes for me. A thunder-shower veiled the horizons at lunch-time, then the sun came out warm and brilliant as we set off on our drive into the Powys and Hardy country.

I had never been greatly excited when riding through pretty scenery, but this trip was different. I felt both elated and awed when we entered Dorset. The view beyond the car windows resembled south Cornwall except that there were more sheep and more thatched cottages here: it was the literary spell that made it all so unique and pregnant. Tess's Blackmore Vale . . . Mr Weston's Folly Down. . . . The car zigzagged amid a maze of chalky lanes and at last drew up close to the window of a small, bare, single-storey building—the Rectory Lodge at Mappowder. I recognised the place from a snapshot Monica had sent me; and as we climbed out and I put Spark down on the bumpy ground, T. F. Powys himself appeared in the door-way and stepped across to greet us, his ruddy, clean-shaven face beaming with a true countryman's welcome. Although seventy-five, he was erect and robust, like a farmer, dressed with casual tidiness in a dark suit. His curly white hair grew thick but not abnormally long on his massive skull. There was something warm and rounded about him: my mother said afterwards that he was "like a child lost in happiness, not thinking of what he was doing". He kissed her hand, and I felt his own hand trembling with emotion as he took mine and led me towards the door. I picked up Spark, and when we got inside the house Powys' adopted daughter Susan came forward smiling and began to pat and stroke Spark's head. She loved animals and worked on a farm, though she had also read a great deal and wore glasses. I then shook hands with Mrs Powys—a homely, practical village woman.

Sitting on the settee with my mother, I realised how appro-priate it was that my first personal contact with literary eminence should come in this unpolished "foreign" outpost instead of among the Cornish dons. I had no prejudice against the academic world, for my work had been honoured in that world for two years past, but I felt more at home in this little lodge where the main room served as lounge, study and dining-room, just as in my cottage at Goonamarris. Powys had not acquired a large library: there were no more books in the room than in the homes of many intelligent village tradesmen. I sat relaxed, absorbing the atmosphere of contentment. We showed Theodore some photographs of me on the clay-tips and outside my garden wall, and he seemed thrilled by their stark simplicity. I wished I could hear the talk, though it was obvious that most of it was gossip between Monica and Mrs Powys. The latter was soon bustling around, laying a plain meal, during which Theodore soaked bread-and-butter in his tea, excusing himself (as I recorded in my poem "Wessex and Lyonnesse") with a whimsical comment about Jesus' action at the Last Supper. There was some discussion of our work, and Powys remarked to my mother: "Jack's books have had a lot of praise—mine were burned by the librarian at Dorchester" (in the 1920s). Mother admitted that many Cornish people disliked my realism, and he observed emphatically that such criticism should be ignored, since it only came from those who didn't understand. He was probably amused when Mother added that she couldn't understand *Mr Weston's Good Wine* at first, "but when Jack explained it to me an' brought out the sermon in it I liked it better". She told him how often I had turned to his books—especially *Soliloquies of a Hermit*—in times of spiritual darkness, and he said quietly: "He turned to my books because he found himself there."

The visit lasted only a couple of hours and we were reluctant to leave the lodge, but Monica's plan had certainly produced one of the most memorable experiences of my life. I knew that I had not merely paid a call on a writer whom I admired: the poet in me was aware of symbolism and pattern, of fitting gestures at a spiritual and emotional frontier where the horizon somehow pulsed with destiny. Powys stood talking with my mother for several minutes outside the house before Monica joined us. He enquired about Mother's religious upbringing and spoke of his own pious mother, saying he always thought of her when he prayed. It was a deep, sober close to our contact. I called a heartfelt "Thank you" as the car moved off in the evening sunshine. My faith, including my confidence about my marriage, was strangely quickened, fused with the warm mellow peace of the Dorset countryside. We climbed Bulbarrow later and were photographed on Sturminster Newton bridge, and there seemed to be no trace of Hardy's tragic irony around his hills and rivers. I described my feelings in the poem "Daybreak in Dorset":

"Fate-ridden land, in Hardy's view,
  Yet every mood I have seen today
On Dorset's face, each passionate hue,
Puts my bleak fate away.
I am purged now
 Even of my purgation: the furnace fires
Are hot in Cornwall, and cold is the sand,
But I take the gentler vow
To sun that ripens when the fierce flame tires."

By the time we reached Sherborne the moon had come up, nearly full, and the old town lay quiet and cloistered in a flutter of pale beams. The dinner at Littleton Powys' elegant Quarry House was not an anti-climax. The glow of release still flooded me and irradiated everything else—Littleton himself, taller than Theodore but frail and half-crippled with arthritis, and his mother-in-law, Mrs Myers, a cheerful, sensitive woman who had borne much suffering. Littleton proudly showed us his sister Gertrude's portrait of Elizabeth Myers, who had died three years before in her early thirties. He was profoundly grateful that in his old age he had married this remarkable girl—a Roman Catholic nature mystic whose novel *A Well Full of Leaves* had been condemned as pantheistic by her priest. I tried to feel her wayward spirit there in the house with her mother and husband, and wished she were still alive: the day would have had a startlingly vivid end if Elizabeth Myers had been able to hand me her scribbled thoughts in a conversation. But she could have added nothing to what Eileen had taught me, and the persistence of the key themes—nature, the Church, exceptional marriage—was obvious enough even in her absence.

CHAPTER SIX

FINGERS AT THE LOCKS

BACK IN CORNWALL, I lived for several weeks in the prophetic glow which I had seen on the Wessex hills and the teeming, dreaming valleys of the Stour, then as the first autumn winds howled around Goonvean clay-pit the sharp grey grip of my old environment reasserted itself and I was bewildered. The writing of the exuberant "Daybreak in Dorset" was followed by the chastened mood of the incident recorded later in "Exit", a poem which describes how I stumbled along the railway line behind Slip quarry, tearing up a postcard Monica had sent me—a message indicating that I was unlikely to meet the Powyses again, and that she could not give me any further introductions that might make my return to Dorset even more enriching from the standpoint of my romantic hopes. She had invited me to come to Church Farm alone, just for a rest and change, at any time, but I felt that this would be an anticlimax. I seemed to be back where I was when Eileen dropped me. The usual cramped life at Goonamarris went on: my mother looked after me and prayed, and my foster-sisters gave me some fun and affection.

Yet the "radiance rare and fathomless" had been real enough on that August journey. I was away from Cornwall only three days, but the emotional and psychological effects were momentous. I had not merely enjoyed my first holiday east of the Tamar; I had received a new, almost a psychic, assurance that my frustration and loneliness, the whole process of being refined through suffering, were temporary and superficial, that pain was not the true keynote of my life or work. It was as if I knew that when I next entered Dorset my wife would be with me. I had made a characteristic gesture of faith at Monica's farm. At my request she had telephoned a Sherborne bookshop and asked that a Church of England Prayer Book should be delivered at Littleton Powys' house for me to collect. A Dorset Prayer Book, I thought, would be a perfect epitome of my transition. I wished to read the Litany which Theodore Powys and the rector had used in Mappowder church, and I wanted even more to become familiar with the Anglican Marriage Service. I had never seen or heard it, for the only wedding I had attended—that of my cousin, Raymond Greenslade, at St Stephen's in 1939—was a simple Methodist one.

Brought up in strict Nonconformity, I was, at thirty-four, as ignorant of church liturgy as an irreligious outsider. I had no idea what Lent was or when it began. I had learnt something of the Apostles' Creed from Barth's *Dogmatics in Outline*, but I did not know the Nicene Creed or the Athanasian Creed. Any recitation of beliefs, except in the form of Biblical texts, was regarded as superstition by sturdy working-class Methodists in my childhood: to them a Prayer Book was almost as idolatrous as a rosary. But my mother's sympathies had broadened in recent years. We had received much kindness from the local rector, Canon Gilbert, who had obtained funds to pay my fares to Plymouth hospital in 1935, and later recommended my books in his parish magazine. In 1949 we bought a radio, and though Mother thought most of the religious programmes "a bit too churchy" she did not object to them, and was therefore not horrified when I proudly set my Sherborne Prayer Book on the shelf beside my Browning volumes.

The little red-backed manual of ecclesiastical worship was a pleasant irony in relation to the literary task which was my chief occupation during that summer. C. Day Lewis, who was then my publishers' adviser, had asked me to prepare a collection of poems which could be issued as a stop-gap following the firm's rejection of my adapted novel. For several months I had been building up the manuscript of *The Clay*

Verge, including all the violent anti-church and anti-nature poems which I had already outgrown. I tried to balance these by putting in revised versions of some of my quieter pre-war pieces, and also the more human and tender love poems I had written since Mother visited London. The complete manuscript contained forty poems, but when I sent it to my publishers they used a drastic blue pencil on it, weeding out twenty-three poems which they regarded as immature or redundant or not in keeping with the special flavour of the best poems. They—or perhaps Day Lewis—evidently wished the aesthetic tone of the whole book to be harsh and sombre, so that it stood up like a lonely splintered crag in a thunderstorm, without a single gay flower or smiling sunbeam. Everything that suggested a colourful and comfortable response to life was cut out. This troubled me because I felt that the seventeen poems that remained in the collection did not give a true or fair picture of me or my beliefs as they were in 1950. Many of the excluded poems appeared in my later volumes, and after I welded some of them into *The Wintry Priesthood*, which had a mass circulation in the Penguin *Poems 1951*, I was glad that they were not kept in *The Clay Verge*, which sold only 180 copies in five years.

My correspondence with Helena Charles had run parallel with the discussion about the Powyses, the ballet girls and fox-hunts of Monica Hutchings' world, but I had said little to Miss Charles regarding my poetry. Her letters often brought unexpected points arising from my prose books. She had given copies of them to various people in her sector of the Church, and informed me of their reactions. A nun friend of hers in an Anglican convent thought I still had much to learn from Catholic mystics. A clergyman missionary home on furlough from South Africa was worried about my Calvinism, and Miss Charles had told him she felt sure that, whatever the Dutch Calvinist churches might do in South Africa, I would *not* use the doctrine of election to support or condone the political and racial policy of apartheid. I could not, in 1950, go far to oblige the nun : I was too frustrated, and too conscious of celibacy as a denial of my vocation, to understand the ascetic teaching of

Thomas à Kempis or St John of the Cross. But I could reassure the missionary: I had always detested racial discrimination as an insult to the absolute freedom in which God chooses His instruments among all classes and colours, making an elect black man like Prophet Harris superior to a non-elect white man like Frank Harris.

Miss Charles, however, was not only concerned about her Church friends' reaction to my work. She was anxious that I should write more prose books and was therefore troubled because of my handicaps, which she knew were beginning to hinder me as a prose writer. I had not heard a conversation since the war, and found it hard to invent spontaneous dialogue. My last short story, "The Clay-dump", was written about this time for an anthology of Cornish stories, but it was based on a discarded chapter of a pre-war novel. I still wrote freely with a fountain-pen in my usual tiny handwriting, but my eyes were easily inflamed by sun or wind, and in this condition the sight became slightly fogged. Treatment had checked but not cured the malady, and when Miss Charles offered to link me with her Church's ministry of healing—for the Anglican authorities were quite willing to accept me as a patient, though not as a teacher—I agreed. I was obviously facing a crisis, and could not afford to neglect any Christian methods that might help.

At first—several months before I visited Dorset—Miss Charles had my name placed on the lists of a few prayer fellowships, then she took me and my mother to a morning Mass at her parish church near Redruth. As Mother and I were heretics we had to sit well back from the mysteries of the altar, mere spectators of the rites. About half-a-dozen communicants went up to the robed, genuflecting priest and had wafers put into their mouths while the candle-light and the sunbeams struggled to say different things about God. I felt the hush of sanctity, the continuity of rituals that were performed through the centuries unchanged by the veerings of secular thought and history, yet there seemed to be no kinship between this specialised, boxed-in religion and the rugged open-air faith that had grown in me as I read my Bible on tank walls and gravel-peaks. After the Mass the vicar came back to my pew, laid his hands on my head and recited a short prayer. There was no trace of emotion: the act appeared to be aloof and perfunctory from my fervent Nonconformist standpoint. But the vicar did not claim to have any gift of healing: this contact was just an initiation, a prelude.

In the spring of 1951 Miss Charles' plans became more ambitious and exciting. She heard that Archbishop William Temple had commissioned a blind man called Godfrey Mowatt to conduct healing services in London. Mowatt had been blinded in childhood by an accidental knife-wound, and had developed psychic powers which he used within the orthodox Church tradition. He was well-known for his quiet but often physically effective ministrations at St Martin-in-the-Fields. Miss Charles, realising my aversion to crowds, suggested that she should try to arrange a private session in which the blind healer might be able to transmit energy that would preserve my sight. I hesitated for a long while, and had many talks with my mother, before I told Miss Charles that I might consent to go to London for such a purpose if the details could be satisfactorily worked out. I might not have agreed to the proposal at all if a letter bearing an Exeter address had not arrived at my home in June and set my thoughts racing back to the previous Christmas and the previous autumn with the same sort of tantalising speculations as I had centred on Eileen.

The letter was from T, a local girl who had attended my old school and chapel at Trethosa but was now at an Exeter college training to be an English teacher. My mother had known her since she was a young child, and they had often come up the twisting lane from the chapel together on Sunday mornings. I was aware from Mother's remarks that this daughter of a clay-labourer was an unusual person, not only clever but deeply religious, solitary, with a dreamy, far-away look in her dark eyes. Her parents had given her a copy of *Wilding Graft*, and its grey unworldliness, which repelled people who associated romantic love with social gaiety, had made a strong emotional appeal to her. She was obviously cast in a mould very similar to mine, and when, soon after going to college (and just as my Dorset glow was fading), she wrote to my mother, telling her how she was adapting herself to the new life, I had sent her a note expressing my understanding of her problems and thanking her for her appreciation of my work, the way her insight had relieved the loneliness I felt in a materialistic working-class community.

She had not answered my letter, but during the Christmas vacation she and her sister called at my home one evening. I shook hands with a tall, slender, dark-haired girl of eighteen who had an air of stillness and hesitation, softly remote from vivacity and gush as she greeted me. She was soon seated on the sofa, and after handing her my press-cuttings album I watched her bend over it, scanning the reviews and occasionally glancing up to make some comment to my mother. I said little, but when she had gone my whole inner world was awed and tremulous. I knew that I was drawn to her, yet the prospects were chilled by her college career and my handicaps. Fear of repeating the Eileen pattern deterred me from writing to her again, and the winter dragged on in confusion. I did practically nothing except enter *The Wintry Priesthood* for a Festival of Britain poetry contest organised by the Arts Council.

Then with the summer flowers and scents came the surprise of T's letter. She had seen an announcement that my sequence of poems had been awarded an Arts Council prize of £100, and sent her warm congratulations. She shyly confessed that she had written a lot of verse herself, and added: "I am sure poetry is inspired, a divine gift from God, though all poets have not recognised it as such." Abruptly she turned to a different subject, oddly linked with Miss Charles' plans. She had recently heard a sermon on faith-healing, which had strengthened her belief that miraculous cures still happened. . . . I replied at greater length this time, telling her that the Arts Council had invited me to come to London to attend a cocktail party which was being thrown for the prize-winning poets. I couldn't imagine *her* at a cocktail party. We were both out of step with sophisticated culture, but we had our compensations. Yes, I believed in spiritual healing . . . and, incidentally, there had been a misprint in the papers about my age: I was only thirty-five yet. . . . She did not continue the correspondence. I was left wondering and a bit disappointed, and as the weeks passed my personal crisis grew darker.

In August I had a day-trip with my mother and foster-sisters to Tintagel and Boscastle, the scenes of Hardy's courtship. I recalled the Dorset hills and pastures and still felt immune from the tragic doom of a Jude. There were happy moments, the girls and I playing leap-frog on Tintagel Head and tramping along the edge of the narrow rocky inlet of Boscastle harbour. But when we arrived home I found bad news awaiting me, as it had awaited me on my return from Falmouth two years before. My agent had at last decided that my revised novel was unsaleable and was therefore posting the typescript back to me. The sense of failure was depressing, even though I had just corrected the proofs of *The Clay Verge* and *The Wintry Priesthood* and sent the handwritten manuscript of the latter sequence to the Arts Council for an exhibition. Three days after receiving the agent's letter I was alarmed by a new symptom of eye trouble—a swirl of red sparks that left the sight clouded for a minute or two. I was taken to Truro hospital again, and the specialist gave a gloomy verdict. There was a definite threat of blindness, and though this might develop gradually over the next five years, it would probably come much sooner. I reported the position to Miss Charles, and she assured me that the meeting with Mowatt would take place at an Anglo-Catholic boarding-house in Soho early in October. My sight improved a little: most days I could read without being distracted by sparks. I often read my Sherborne Prayer Book, and was, in fact, reading the Marriage Service on the afternoon of the second Sunday in September when, glancing out of the window, I saw T's tall figure coming up the path.

As soon as she stepped into the room I guessed what had brought her there. She looked strained and worried. I sat subdued, silent for the most part, during the next hour while she talked earnestly with my mother, telling her that she had been very upset on hearing that the doctors had abandoned me to blindness. She wished to do everything she could to help my recovery. God might want to use her in a way that people would not understand. . . . In the evening T stayed with me while my mother and the Allen girls went to chapel. It was strange, being alone with her, and in an atmosphere of anxiety that precluded all normal, light-hearted discussion. She tried to make her attitude clear, jotting brief notes in an attempt to get into conversation with me. But the magnitude of the situation, the knowledge of what Eileen had suffered after I raised the marriage issue, kept me emotionally strangled, afraid of bringing anguish and disillusion on T also. She went home with no advance made even towards a friendship.

On the following Tuesday she returned to the Goonamarris cottage, and now it seemed that it was my reserved and unresponsive manner that distressed her. We prayed for guidance and touched the frontier of a deeply poignant and spiritual attachment. But the day ended in unhappy drama, for her family's reaction, naturally, was the same as that of Eileen's parents. There were confused rumours later, and I never learnt the exact truth about T's motives and decisions. Her relatives must have convinced her that the position was hopeless: she never visited me again, nor did she answer my subsequent letters. She was a gentle and submissive girl, less of a rebel than Eileen: in any case, a girl needs the support of a competent, active, articulate lover if she is to defy the rest of the world in pursuit of a romance. I could not meet her outside my home unless my eyes strengthened. The only remedy was a miracle in Soho, and the shock of losing touch with T at the crucial moment had almost made me incapable of positive faith. I felt dull and heavy when the grey October day came and my mother and I boarded the train at St Austell.

The six hours' journey across England was as much of a strain to Mother as it was to me. She remembered her previous ill-fated visit to London, the fading of my fancy about Irene. Since then she had seen me embark on two mature relationships which had followed the Wimpole Street pattern up to a point and then disintegrated. She was sadly perplexed, but as her mind was not at all speculative or analytical she bore the simple burden of the ordinary believer trying to make sense of "God's will" when circumstances seem to reveal only the power of a cruel fate and the frailty of human nature. She sat grim-faced in the railway carriage, handing me a sandwich or fruit at intervals and patting my arm consolingly when, as we neared London, I grew restless and fretful, my sight misty again because of draughts and dust. I wondered vaguely what the evening would bring. Miss Charles had arranged for an Austrian refugee friend of hers to meet us at Paddington station, get a taxi and go with us to Dean Street, Soho, where Godfrey Mowatt would be awaiting us at the guest-house.

I could hear the din of Paddington only as a faint discord as we climbed wearily out on to the platform, but the place looked bleared and terrifying. A courteous, foreign-featured young man accosted us, and when he grasped my elbow and led me forward I thought in a dazed, flickering sort of way about his background. He was an ex-Roman Catholic who had become an Anglican because, according to Miss Charles, he was so pleased to find that English clergymen did not live in sin. He swung into the front seat of a cab, and I was soon experiencing the nerve-racking jolts, swerves and abrupt standstills of my first taxi ride through the streets of London. The coloured neon-signs and white traffic headlights flashed and vanished in mad scribbles, and when we stepped on to the kerb in Dean Street and all the lights except car-lamps were held steady, it was almost like entering a vacuum.

We were shown into the large boarding-house and introduced to Mowatt—a gaunt elderly man with a human warmth tempering his mystical detachment. He had been married for many years, but a young woman assistant was with him now. We had a leisurely meal, and after further conversation we all filed outdoors again, skirted some blitz rubble and descended a flight of steps into a private chapel or church crypt: in the gloom I could not see exactly what it was. The tension mounted as my mother sank to her knees and drew me down beside her. I closed my eyes and waited, unable to hear the blind man move up behind me. His assistant guided him, and suddenly his big bony hands grasped my head and began to vibrate. I tried to pray, but the spiritual awareness which had brought me such ecstasies on the Cornish clay-tips, and in Dorset, was suffocated here. An absurd spasm of guilt and remorse gripped me, due largely to physical exhaustion and the emotional up-heaval of the past few weeks. God couldn't heal me for T because all my work had been inspired by other girls. If T were the *only* girl in my life, the miracle would happen. Now it was too late. The blind man was wasting his time, fastening his fingers around my skull, pressing, attempting to transmit. . . . I started to cry, the tears splashing down on my sleeves, my slumped body convulsed with sobs. Mowatt continued his un-ruffled prayer, serene in God's presence. At last his hands lifted, and I was helped to my feet, still overwrought, yet struggling to be grateful for the kindness and sacrifice of these people. Miss Charles was praying in Cornwall, and she had paid all our expenses. Mother had joined the intercessors, and it wasn't their fault if I was not receptive.

Back in the cosy lounge, I braced myself and thanked Mowatt as I bade him good-bye. I spent an almost sleepless night in a bedroom cluttered with images of saints. I was too fatigued to think coherently of my London affinities—Browning, Elizabeth Barrett, Donne, Blake. But I knew I was near Wimpole Street, Westminster Abbey and St Paul's Cathedral. I was not far from the church where Browning had spoken his vows, and the streets where Jack Donne had expended his wit and money on whores. . . .

"With my body I thee worship. . . ."

"Burn off my rusts and my deformity. . . ."

The two voices blended and I dozed. Early next morning my mother and I were taken by taxi to Paddington, and the clergy-man who owned the Soho guest-house put us on a Cornwall-bound train. My sight was a little clearer, and now in broad daylight I felt more healthy and hopeful. Mowatt had said that healing was often gradual, and that in some cases God healed the circumstances *without* a physical cure. He himself had remained blind, but he had married the girl he wanted. There would be a way through for me.

CHAPTER SEVEN

THE BED IS STILL BROAD

THE AUTUMN OF 1951 must have been unusually wet, for when I sent a copy of the Penguin volume containing *The Wintry Priesthood* to T. F. Powys in November, he ended his note of thanks with the whimsical comment: "I hope all goes well with you and you are not washed away with all this rain." It was the first time I had contacted him since the week of the Mappowder visit, and this was the last message I received from him. He developed cancer and died two years later, and during that period nothing seemed to go well with me and some of my foundations were almost washed away by a flood of suffering. I posted a copy of the Penguin book to T, and the daily suspense and disappointment as I waited in vain for her reply was hardly the psychological state in which Mowatt's ministration could take effect. I had to tell Miss Charles that I had apparently derived no benefit from the London venture, that the concentrated prayers had neither healed me nor changed T's decision. Miss Charles, with her respect for Catholic asceticism, began to suggest that the denial of my wish for sense-fulfilment might be part of a mystical process in which I must be "stripped of everything but God". I retorted that Elizabeth Barrett had passed through such a process and found that it was just a prelude to wedded bliss.

As an artist, I was still unshaken, for in the midst of all this strain I wrote two of my best poems—"Beyond Trethosa Chapel" and "Reclaimed". Both were inspired by T, the former being concerned with the fusion which her personality could help me to achieve between my individual clay-peak vision and a simple Nonconformist fellowship:

> "Mediate, then, beloved; let tension cease,
> Dune-grit and pews be reconciled. . . .
> Bless with your dreams my broken clay
> As you take the broken bread:
> Fuse the corporate flame with our lonely ray;
> Show me that Bethel wine is red."

This poem was soon accepted by John Lehmann for the *London Magazine*, and by Charles Causley for a West Region BBC poetry programme. The publicity tended to strengthen my hope that T's influence was something more than a final irony. In "Reclaimed" I expressed the same hope in less direct terms, using claywork symbols to describe my present condition as it might seem to Miss Charles:

> "Just the bald blunt pile in winter's grip,
> Flood waters rising as the dune sags. . . ."

But T's bid to rescue me was still the pledge of a triumphant future:

> "Storm-flash of grace has bared my spirit's peak,
> And the scabrous flesh grows sleek,
> While the young breast, immune and sealed
> From fate, lies healed
> In dreams of the reclaiming day."

I always knew that I was stating a Christian faith, not a mere poetic escape into the ideal. Some poets and other artists have driven themselves mad by demanding that objective facts must conform to their own fantastic notions of what life ought to be like. But my belief that I was destined to marry was based on a Christian sense of vocation which had nothing to do with poetic fancies. Spiritually, I did not live in a typical "poet's world". My poetry had firm Evangelical roots which made it tough and realistic, in some ways anti-poetic, though my lavish use of description and imagery showed a poet's vivid sensuous awareness.

Now that my sight was threatened I realised more than ever how much I owed to the sharp receptive powers of my youth— a fact which was already being overlooked by journalists and reviewers. Monica Hutchings had published in the *West Country Magazine* a well-meant but in some respects inaccurate article about me, stating that I was "virtually blind" (though she admitted that I could still read), and that in my teens and twenties my mother had been content that I should do nothing but write. "She never suggested that he should do anything else—make baskets or address envelopes." This implies that I was nearly blind at the time when, in fact, my mother was often urging me to get a job at Goonvean claywork or Slip stone quarry. Monica's article was the beginning of a flood of misrepresentations about my handicaps which was to spread all over Britain during the next two decades. The public was invited to picture me as a sort of Cornish version of Helen Keller. It was a ludicrous legend, and no intelligent reader of my books could have believed it. I had been compared with Hardy because my descriptive passages showed such acute observation, such a keen eye for details of landscape: the effect of cloud-shadows on buildings and rural contours; the ways in which the changing hues of dawn and sunset softened the grim industrial features; the first shafts of daybreak striking the clay-tips, setting the electric wires shimmering like spiders' webs far up against the sky while the gravel slopes remained vague; the last mellow rays of evening light slanting on the wooden tip-beams "so that iron fastenings scarring their dull grained surface were plainly visible from below". Only a clear-sighted author could record such impressions.

My next meeting with Monica Hutchings was not spoilt by complaints about her article, for I knew she had wished to pay the highest tribute to my courage, but the visit was a pale shadow of the earlier one which involved the Dorset magic. In

March 1952 my mother and I spent two nights at Church Farm, using it as a base in connection with a faith-healing service at Malvern. I was still fascinated by the healing ministry, and thought that a Nonconformist approach might suit me better than the Anglican. An American Baptist pastor was holding a service at a Malvern chapel, and I had written to him. Monica and her husband gave us a free trip to the lovely Malvern Hills, and Spark was with us again, but I could only see dim blobs of the countryside, though it lay sharp in winter sunshine. We left Spark with Monica when we reached the church. There was an ordinary service with a sermon, and after the congregation had gone the pastor—a small, cheerfully dynamic man—knelt and held my wrists while he prayed and said that a strong healing current was flowing into me. I felt calm and confident, and was spiritually brighter as we rode back to Somerset, though next morning there was a pang at being unable to cross the border into my enchanted Dorset.

A few days later I wrote to tell Monica that my sight had definitely improved. Each evening after dark I slipped outdoors and stood on the garden edge, looking across the valley at the clay-tank lights and up at the cone-tips of Trethosa and Goonvean, seeing the white flare of the arc-lamps more clearly than I had done for months past. This was encouraging and made me less troubled about variations in my condition, but the partial recovery did not last long: by the autumn I found reading difficult without the aid of a black cardboard line-screen, and only went for short walks alone with Spark. His companionship had become very precious to me, and it was a desolating blow when, early in November, he died in convulsions after a veterinary surgeon had given him injections every day for a fortnight: the deadly "hard pad" disease had not been detected soon enough.

With Spark buried in the garden beside Flush, there was no youthful and lively atmosphere left in the house except when Violet and Frances were present. They had both finished school now and taken jobs as shop assistants. They were quiet and sensible girls, showing no signs of adolescent wildness and rebellion. My mother's warm efficient kindness was so different from anything they had known in Plymouth that they respected her strict Methodist views. They did not drink, smoke or go to dances. They went to St Dennis cinema on Saturdays with girl friends, and sometimes played tennis and other games at Nanpean recreation ground. They spent most of their evenings contentedly at home, often sitting on my knee for a little teasing, or scribbling notes in brief conversations with me. It was pleasant to be in daily contact with girls of fifteen or sixteen, but, as I had surmised at the outset, they never conveyed that indefinable something which an artist recognises as inspiration. The comfort they gave was complete in itself, not a medium for the transcendent, and for me an inspirer had to be a medium. They accepted me in a matter-of-fact way, as they had accepted Aunt Bertha, half proud of me, half sorry for me. They did not read much of my work or connect it with girls, though they knew I had wanted to marry Eileen in 1949 and T in 1951. Frances had remarked to my mother, in the brisk Cornish which had become natural to her: "'Tis a pity the maids let him down."

Whether I had been "let down" or not, I was, at the end of 1952, thin and very grey-haired, looking and feeling prematurely old. I had been idle for most of the year, merely revising my rejected novel and writing a handful of poems. Some of them repeated my confidence in the purpose of the T episode, but these were minor pieces published only in the *Cornish Review*. I had also written "Goonvean Claywork Farm" in tribute to my mother's faith. Here again I affirmed the concept of Browning's "By the Fireside", in which marriage is linked with "the great Word which makes all things new". Referring to the old stable at Goonvean, which was still intact when I composed the poem, though it was demolished soon afterwards, I wrote:

> "The stable spoke of a higher Law,
>   The birth of the Word
>   Who saw you when your fruit was mown

In the mire, and set
Bounds to the clay-waste, won
A new earth for your son."

It is significant that in this poem, the only one inspired by
my mother, I laid all the stress on her religious influence. Up
to 1953 my work was carried on in complete independence of
my mother. She had not always approved of it, and I had
written several novels which she had not found time or inclina-
tion to read. Her practical care and sacrifice in feeding and
clothing me for thirty-six years and supporting me on her own
war widow's pension until 1946 were praiseworthy, but
thousands of mothers had shown such devotion to their sub-
normal, abnormal or cantankerous offspring. My debt was not
simply like that which Sean O'Casey owed to his mother amid
the hardship and squalor of the Dublin slums; it was more like
St Augustine's debt to Monica. My mother had thrown the
whole force of her prayers against my deep-rooted paganism,
knowing that her prayers expressed the will of God while my
paganism expressed only the tragedy of my father's family—a
tragedy of dissipation, cruelty, broken marriages, illegitimate
births and (in the case of my Aunt Hetty) nymphomania. Her
spiritual power had gradually released me, or enabled God to
release me, from this warping background, as far as my
psychological and emotional tendencies were concerned, and
it was on this level that our relationship was rare and disturbing
in the materialistic twentieth century.

Her prayers were now augmented by those of church people
of all denominations, from Miss Charles' brother, a Roman
Catholic, to my elderly cousin, Ern Polmounter, pastor of a
Pentecostal church in America, who came to Cornwall on
holiday in the summer of 1952 and fervently anointed me with
oil as I sat at my desk. I had, of course, told Miss Charles about
my Malvern experience, and she had charitably approved of it.
She had also discovered a Cornish vicar, Father Barnicoat of
St Agnes, who was willing to grant me a regular course of
priestly intercession. I accepted the offer, and from the spring

of 1952 until the summer of 1953 Miss Charles came up from Redruth almost every Friday and took my mother and me to the quaint little church which held its slim spire high between derelict tin-mines and the granite cliffs that curved massively down towards St Ives.

As I saw Father Barnicoat only in the gloom of his church, I have no clear memory of his appearance. He was ageing and of medium build, wore a hearing-aid and sometimes seemed a little reserved, heavily self-conscious about his priestly office. He was genuinely anxious to help me, and had no doubt that these frequent pilgrimages to St Agnes would convince me that the Church was my true spiritual home. During the 1952 sessions I merely sat relaxed and receptive, open to the religious atmosphere of the shadowy pillars, while he laid his hands on my head and prayed. But this could not continue indefinitely, and early in 1953 he suggested a final and fully sacramental ministration in which he would use oil that had been consecrated by the Bishop of Truro. He explained that before this could be done I would need the preliminary Catholic rite of confession and absolution. I hesitated for weeks over this proposal: both the Nonconformist and the poet in me were uneasy, afraid that in my search for healing I was compromising too much, going too far into an alien climate or clutter of formalities. But in the end I agreed, regarding the act as a wholesome gesture of humility and not a slavish and superstitious submission to priestcraft. The ritual took place just before the Coronation of Queen Elizabeth. I knelt in the semi-darkness of the cool sanctuary and told Father Barnicoat all the sins I could remember having committed. He then pronounced the Church's absolution, and I felt the holy oil trickle down my forehead. There was a divine presence, the same profound love and mystery that I had so often known on the clay-tips, but in a different medium.

That, however, was for me the end of the Anglo-Catholic road. My sight and hearing did not improve, and Miss Charles once more stressed her view that "all these disasters"—the persistent handicaps, the fiasco of my Trethosa "romance", the frustration of my work—seemed to indicate that my rôle on the earthly stage was that of a sufferer, a man sustained by grace alone, with all natural pleasures mortified. My vocation might be higher, more akin to Christ's bitter cup, than I had supposed. She pointed me to Bernadette instead of Elizabeth Barrett. But I remained incorrigible, and wrote back stubbornly: "I want my Christian friends to share my own buoyant confidence in the God Who 'giveth us richly all things to enjoy'. I do not at all share your emphasis on suffering. There is a truer revelation of God in the least happiness than in years of misery." Miss Charles must have sighed, but she could do nothing further for me, so our correspondence ceased. I never learnt anything of her subsequent life, but I was grateful for her generosity, and she had widened my spiritual and aesthetic horizons.

The "fiasco" about T had become an open defeat before I lost touch with Miss Charles. I had been told that T was developing a friendship with a fellow student, and one Sunday evening my mother saw her at Trethosa chapel with this young man. It was a painful shock, though after nearly two years' silence we might have expected ironies of this sort to accompany the broadcasting and publication of "Beyond Trethosa Chapel" (then called simply "Trethosa Chapel"). I was already in a state of physical and emotional exhaustion which, but for the healing ministry, might have led to a nervous breakdown or something worse. In the autumn of 1953 I was weakened by heart trouble, severe palpitation and fluttering, and attacks of cerebral paralysis in which I was semi-conscious for hours. Doctors said it was an aftermath crisis following the long courses of injections I had received at hospitals, and that it could prove fatal. Grimly I held on while the floods pounded. I was fighting for life—and still fighting towards marriage. The only poem I composed in 1953 was "Clay Phoenix", which I dictated to my mother one Monday morning when I was too ill to write. The poem began by portraying the feelings of a jilted lover, and culminated in mystical speculations about marriage in relation to death and the resurrection of the body.

The opening lines were misconstrued by some critics, who thought I was referring to physical blindness—a subject I would never bother to write about except as an incidental complication of religious or erotic problems. The "quenched wires" were not my eyes but my hopes of marrying T.

> "I am far down in the pit and blinded
>   By the ambiguous flash: where the signals loomed
>   All is dark. Am I now entombed?
>   No, for I did not descend
>   A narrow shaft for my truth:
>   The bed is still broad, exposed to the changeful sky. . . ."

Since this poem came to me in such desperate circumstances, it embodies my faith in its most elemental form. There is no trace of a churchy influence; the symbols are those of fire, wind and rain on the clayworks. Apparently my imagination had not yet absorbed the new sacerdotal world which could mean ecstasy or soul-storm under spires and belfries. Memories of my childhood and youth were more easily trusted: indeed, it was not until nearly twenty years later, after my marriage, that I was able to write poems describing my experiences in Soho and at St Agnes. My fierce individualism had affirmed Christianity in most of my mature poems, so I could not renounce it as a pagan force like the early individualism of Donne and Eliot. I had to draw subtle distinctions between egotism and idiosyncrasy, between personal aberration and personal idiom. Above the clay-pit and the church tower was the same "changeful sky", which had smiled so benevolently in the summer of 1950 and was now hurling thunderbolts and torrents. I had bought my Sherborne Prayer Book in order to read the Marriage Service and the Litany, and now, in November of this Coronation year, the Burial Service had been used for T. F. Powys. Monica Hutchings wrote to tell me about the simple, moving funeral at Mappowder, and I thought it a strange coincidence that my fellow hermit-mystic should die at the time when doctors feared that I had not long to live.

I had obviously reached the end of a phase. T, Miss Charles, Theodore Powys—all had been withdrawn, and only a new phase could show how much of what they stood for was still valid for me.

CHAPTER EIGHT

A DIFFERENT FACE

THE CORNISH CLAY district is almost a mountain region. Its highest outcrop, the long twisted knuckle of Hensbarrow Downs, rises over a thousand feet above sea level, taking the brunt of hurricanes and giving magnificent views far beyond the industrial belt. My home was on a slightly lower ridge to the west, but it was fiercely buffeted by gales that swept in from both coasts, and the north wind howling down from Bodmin Moor. Standing at my bedroom window as a child, I could scan twenty miles of countryside sloping away to Truro (which was hidden in a hollow) and on to the squat sullen tor of Carn Brea, and sometimes when the weather was clear I would catch a glint of sunlight on the Channel, ten miles to the south. As a result of this geographical elevation, I grew up with a great liking for winds and wide horizons. A poet's mind and emotional pitch are affected by altitude as well as heredity. Had I always lived in a sheltered dale with a cramped view, my writings might have been less tough and complex. A sensitive dweller on the heights is more conscious of solitude as an aid to vision. He is also more aware of violence, of the need to protect himself and his stores against hostile elements.

Whether it was through the daily contemplation of lower land from a hilltop, or through the romanticised misery of feeling myself cut off and degraded by the "ancestral mesh" of pagan Clemos, I was never able to get anywhere near the outlook of people who lived on the average level. I was never a boy playing happily with other boys, or an adolescent sharing the interests of other teenagers. In my later schooldays I had occasionally gone at midday to the home of my aunt, Annie Greenslade, on Trethosa Downs, and after I had eaten the dinner which my mother brought there for me I would go with Raymond to fetch milk from a farm in the valley. While we descended the broad open scarp and passed through a gateway into the farm lane, Raymond would be chattering about a football match or the camping exploits of local Scouts, but though I liked him well enough—he was a serious, reliable lad, a year or two my senior—I listened with stupefaction rather than mere boredom and made no response. Nor did I fare better when we reached the farm and a gaunt, grinning young woman cracked jokes as she tipped milk from a can into Raymond's jug. Her jokes didn't get through to me any more than my cousin's talk: I would turn away unsmiling, sealed off in a world of my own.

The psychological barrier may have been widened by the spell of semi-blindness I suffered when I was five, but there was a deeper isolation, that of the poet and mystic, which could not have been produced by the temporary inflammation of an eye. The loneliest years of my life were the physically un-handicapped years of adolescence, for I then had no screen to shield me from the direct impact of a community whose values were a menace to my ideals. Seeing all around me the coarse, jeering or jovial faces of materialistic villagers, hearing their crude gossip about sports or the local pig club or somebody "gittin'" double the money 'e 'ad in 'is old job—'is wife lookin' some swish in 'er new rig-out she bought for Easter", I could only creep away among the silent rocks of a quarry like a wounded animal, or sit brooding amid the tar and cobwebs in a claywork shed. Trivial chatter was all the talk I got even from the girl who inspired my mystical verse, and this made the irony unbearable. It was during this period that I felt most piercingly the truth of Blake's words:

"O why was I born with a different face?
    Why was I not born like the rest of my race?

When I look, each one starts; when I speak I offend;
When I'm silent and passive I lose every friend."

I have to stress this solitude of temperament because I have now reached the point in my story where, if the legend about me were correct, I would have felt a greater loneliness arising from the slow failure of my sight. In actual fact, my next book showed that as my sight receded my sense of loneliness receded also. *The Invading Gospel* is buoyant with the glow of fellowship, the exuberance of a man who has identified himself with a popular cause and is unconscious that he is in any way cut off from the herd—at least, from the herd of singing converts at evangelistic rallies. It was no wonder that D. S. Savage, after visiting me early in 1954, described me in a broadcast as "the most paradoxical personality in Cornwall". While my sight was good I had written books which expressed a harsh uncompromising withdrawal from social life, but now that I could only see people as blurred shapes I seemed to have become a very friendly and gregarious writer, full of the Chestertonian gusto that made a reviewer compare *The Invading Gospel* with *Orthodoxy*.

How far was this a genuine development, a growth in grace, and how far was it the result of a desperate clutch at something that looked big enough to support me at a time when the floods were trying to tear up all my roots? It was certainly a new phase, as remote as anything could be from the rural musings of T. F. Powys and the solemn traditional rituals of Helena Charles. What matters now about my so-called "revivalist" phase is that it gave me a fresh grip on life and fresh inspiration for work, thus filling a gap before the next crisis in my search for marriage brought me back to erotic poetry.

I was thankful that I could still read, for in the spring of 1954 I read in the *Methodist Recorder* John Betjeman's balanced appreciation of the Billy Graham crusade in London. This made me feel that I hadn't really disgraced myself as an artist by allowing the religious excitement aroused by the campaign to invigorate me. I myself could never have been converted through mass evangelism: I had to take the artist's lonely road to the Cross, working through private symbols and analogies to theological fact. But T. S. Eliot had declared that Donne was a Billy Sunday type of religious spellbinder, and this had made Donne even more fascinating to me. I never had much kinship with poets who were mere artists: such a neat and easy classification repelled me. I demanded a riddle, a baffling mixture, so that the fastidious poet was also a fervid preacher, a hard-hitting controversialist, a social or political firebrand. Art, to me, was not a cause to be served, but only a way in which people with a certain kind of brain could serve causes, and the decision as to which cause art served must be made outside the aesthetic sphere: it was determined by spiritual and moral awareness of man's predicament. My books showed that my awareness was very close to that of evangelists. *Wilding Graft* was a novel about conversion, and the blurb on my first collection of poems claimed that they revealed "how violent can be the struggle between fallen man and his redeeming God". It was therefore not surprising that I should be deeply moved by the most spectacular evangelistic campaign which had ever been held in England.

During the grey days of March I strained my eyes to read reports of the Harringay meetings and the testimonies of converts, several of which vindicated my basic theme—the transformation of sexual behaviour and marriage by divine grace. Sometimes when my heart felt weak I would lounge on the settee for hours with the crusade song-book in my hands. The Sankey hymns brought back memories of Trethosa chapel as it was in my childhood. The tunes were still vivid in my mind, as I had often heard them on gramophone records during the war, before severe deafness became chronic with me in 1945. I scrawled in my diary: "I seem to have collapsed into song, which is the nicest way to collapse if one must go through that sort of discipline." Somehow the song sharpened into an urge to set down a statement of the faith that was keeping me optimistic in circumstances which would have made many people commit suicide. (There were, in fact, half-a-dozen suicides in the surrounding villages during the years in which I was going blind, most of them due to money troubles or poor health.) Before the London crusade closed in the mammoth rally at Wembley Stadium I had jotted a few thousand words of *The Invading Gospel*.

From the outset the production of this book was incredibly difficult. I could no longer see clearly enough to write legibly in normal style; I had to "print" each letter separately. I found also that the material did not come to me in an orderly sequence. I had so much to say about so many different subjects that my notebooks were soon a chaotic jumble of fragments. Nothing of this could be typed until I had sorted it out and built up a complete chapter, and in any case I could not type it myself. I had never learnt touch-typing, but like many male authors I had gained fair speed and accuracy in typing by sight with my forefingers. Now the keys were too indistinct. My mother had begun typing my letters while I sat beside her and dictated them. She was sixty in 1954, and had never typed a line in the past, and as she was often tired after her housework she made almost as many mistakes as I would have done. She was doubtful about spelling and at first very slow in picking out the right keys. We sometimes struggled for an hour to get a hundred words typed. There was no possibility of her typing the book. Yet we felt strangely confident that the thoughts that kept flashing through my mind would eventually get published.

The stimulus of working on my *credo* brought me a new wave of physical energy, strengthening my heart and clearing my brain. I had no more prostrating attacks after June. I was also cheered to receive a second grant from the Royal Literary Fund, and new friends among West Country writers were encouraging me. D. S. Savage, whom I had seen dimly as a tallish bearded figure, had published an essay on my poetry in America, and in the letters he sent me from his home at Mevagissey he mingled praise with caution, urging me to be on guard against a swing of the pendulum. I had been a strongly individual artist in my early work, and must not degenerate into a commonplace tub-thumper. . . . The Devon critic and sociologist, E. W. Martin—a short stocky man, nervous in manner but forceful in his opinions—had also visited me, with his cultured wife, Elisabeth. He, too, was a little worried lest my grey and craggy mysticism should be spoilt by the glamour and flamboyance of revivalists.

But my behaviour on another front proved that I was as stubbornly idiosyncratic as ever. Since 1952 I had been getting routine calls from welfare officers who wished to teach me Braille and the manual alphabet and take me to clubs and parties for the handicapped. They were appalled to find me, as it seemed, a cantankerous hermit who refused all help and was determined to deal with handicaps in a way that suited his own sense of values. Mother spent hours trying to explain my faith in divine intervention and the fulfilment of intuitions which God "whispers in the ear". The ladies listened politely on the whole, but occasionally one of them would make an exasperated comment such as: "He's just being obstinate—he simply won't face his position," or "He's just like the Christian Scientists—pretending the problem isn't there." And when the winter of 1954–55 closed in, my mother was inclined to fear that the ladies might be correct. She saw me slumped uselessly at my desk on dull days, unable to read or write until the electric light was switched on. At such times she could only communicate with me by tracing block letters on my palm with her finger-tip. Wouldn't my mind be more alert if I used Braille and the quick conversational medium of manual signs? I replied that it was my actual physical condition which had made Eileen and T drop me: neither of them, nor their parents' attitude, would have been changed by my learning a few tricks from welfare officers. I wasn't interested in the petty mechanical business of "overcoming handicaps". Braille couldn't open up the way to the fulfilment I had written about. I must concentrate on the unseen forces, the spiritual and psychological laws that could still create the Wimpole Street pattern for me.

A more conventional kind of courtship was already going on in our cottage, for Violet had fallen in love with a Nanpean clayworker called Morley—a huge, good-looking young fellow of solid character, an enthusiastic footballer but with no taste for pubs or dance-halls. He and Violet became engaged in 1954 and he called at our home two or three times a week to take her out, frequently having a meal with us. At Christmas I had seen their blurred forms diving and bouncing on the settee as they laughed and scuffled for the possession of some nuts. I had often frolicked in similar fashion with schoolgirls, but this was different and I felt a pang at the reminder of what was still missing in my life. The wedding preparations started soon after Violet's nineteenth birthday at the beginning of 1955. Mother tried to be cheerful for Violet's sake, but when she was alone with me she seemed burdened and perplexed. Hadn't she waited long enough for *my* wedding? I did not attend the ceremony at St Austell, but I saw Violet, slim and calm in her white bridal dress and veil, as she gave me a swift kiss and hurried out to the car, carrying her bouquet. She lived for a while with Morley's family, the Craddocks, then the pair moved to a house of their own at St Dennis, two miles away. Frances felt the loss of her sister very keenly, as she herself had not yet got involved with a young man, and the atmosphere of our cottage was at times painfully emotional. I was living with an ageing mother and a frustrated girl of eighteen whose own mother was dead, and we all wanted the situation to change.

In the brilliant summer weather I could read and write for longer periods, though reading was difficult unless I held the print in the direct track of sunlight with my black line-screen cutting off dazzle. I read books and magazines on evangelism and the healing ministry—nothing of much literary value except the Bible and Prayer Book. I had to preserve a climate of positive faith. Nearly half of *The Invading Gospel* was written by the autumn, but chiefly as a mass of bits and pieces scattered through exercise books. I had produced no poems since "Clay Phoenix", and had no wish to write more poetry. I was using my talents on a controversial, propaganda level, following Milton, who had laid poetry aside for years in order to hurl pamphlets into the battle for religious and civil liberty. Though I had always found *Paradise Lost* unreadable, it was a comfort to think of Milton, for, in middle age, after he had gone blind, he had married a girl, believing that the Almighty had elected him for chaste pleasures, not tragic loneliness. His modified Calvinism resembled mine—the concept of election without the chilling fiat of reprobation: the troublesome misfit fulfilling his pact with God, but functioning inside the broad frame of universal grace. Milton had also been disillusioned about the churches and ended as a non-churchgoing Christian, having fellowship at home with friends of various denominations.

My closest Christian friend at this time was the local Methodist minister, the Rev. Gordon Turner. He often came down from the St Dennis manse to visit us, and sometimes performed the simple rite of the Lord's Supper in our lounge. He was a tall, pale young man who took his vocation very seriously and believed that God had prepared him for it through much trial and sorrow. His first fiancée had died and he had married her sister. Their first child had died and their second had a long and dangerous illness in infancy. Then in 1954 Gordon himself was stricken with thrombosis and lay at death's door in hospital for days. I prayed desperately for him, thinking of his wife and baby. He recovered and resumed his duties, but he never looked robust. Some of the chapel people thought his afflictions had warped him, made him stern and puritanical. I found his single-minded devotion and earnestness a welcome contrast to the easy-going humanism of many ministers. He was cautious about mass evangelism, fearing that most of its results were superficial, lacking the spiritual agony that really identified a convert with Christ. He greatly admired my early work, but was a little perplexed when Mother told him that my circumstances had now become so black that I was writing a very cheerful book in reaction against the pious view that all misfortunes are blessings in disguise. He knew about T's attempt to liberate me, and felt that she had probably acted on a mere religious and emotional impulse. "If it was God's will, nothing could have stopped it," he said.

This point was bothering me a lot as I tried to formulate a rational theological basis for my book. My failure to win either

Eileen or T had rid me of all cocksureness about God's will being the established fact at *every* stage of one's life. Christ had wept over Jerusalem, so He might still weep when human free will caused needless suffering. Yet the idea of a loving but defeated God was no more satisfactory than the idea of a despotic and cruel one. The Bible could not straighten out the problem, since it contained statements in support of both views. I could understand the hard-bitten sceptic who claims that religious people get themselves into a hopeless muddle of time-wasting speculations, and that the only sensible course is to make the best of life as it is, asking no questions about a divinity that shapes or fails to shape a transcendent pattern. But such a brisk solution is obviously an evasion of evidence, for life as it is includes the testimony of the vindicated believer who can say, as Browning said in a love letter to Elizabeth Barrett: "So it has ever been in my life of wonders—absolute wonders, with God's hand over all." Despite the baffling enigmas, the vast stretches of ignorance, the swift and stunning ironies which can follow an apparent miracle, I could only accept the fact that I was still undefeated, that at some point in the testing I had seen in the eyes of God not a tear but a twinkle.

That twinkle was certainly hidden as the autumn of this fateful year drew on and the mists and grey skies distorted my last dim glimpses of the clay-dumps. It was clear that the struggle to retain my eyesight was nearly over. Before Christmas the white phosphorescent fog (caused by damaged blood-cells at the back of the eyes) had become too thick for me to see any print through it even in sunshine. I could still distinguish objects out of the corner of my left eye, and continued to do so for another two years, but as far as reading and writing were concerned I ended 1955 in total blindness.

CHAPTER NINE

THE WHITE PRISON

THERE IS A tradition that the Cornish Clemos are descendants of a French family called Clement who escaped from France to Cornwall soon after the massacre of St Bartholomew's Day in 1572. The young male Clements married Cornish girls, and as they did not pronounce the "t" in their name it eventually got into the registers as Clemo. I was middle-aged before this item of ancestral history reached me from various sources, and apart from feeling pleased that I might have in my veins the blood of religious rebels and refugees I was not much impressed by the information. It could not explain why I am so distressingly different from the other Cornish Clemos. As far as I know, I am the first member of the family who has shown a contrast of qualities that could have resulted from a mixture of Gallic and Celtic blood. The French are supposed to be clear, logical thinkers, and they are supposed to understand sex. The Celts are alleged to be primitive, full of wild mystical intuitions, so that they become melancholy dreamers when their more ferocious tendencies are not being provoked. I possess the characteristics of both groups, yet my father and grandfather seemed, in their mental and emotional capacity, typical of thousands of English labourers brought up in Victorian slum conditions.

The old Clemo cottage was one of a block of three squalid dwellings almost encircled by the towering white rubble from Trethosa clay-pit. Outside the garden wall was a railway siding flanked by a long line of drying-kilns with their grim stone pillars, wooden awnings and corrugated-iron roofs. The air was foul with clay-dust and the grime of coal trucks coming in from Cardiff. I never felt that my true roots were there and I was not sorry when the whole site was overrun and buried under the gravel-dump during my teens, but as a schoolboy I often ate my midday meal at the cottage, and when I was seven or eight years of age my mother sent me there on one evening each week while I was taking music lessons from my Uncle Horatio. He redeemed the ugliness, bringing song and harmony into the dank, prison-like house. I would creep timidly to the back door, and when my shrivelled, rasping old grandmother had let me in I crossed the bare flagstones of the kitchen floor, parted the heavy red curtains that screened the passage and entered the tiny parlour. It was a musician's den, with an organ close to the door, a violin and accordion on the sofa, mouth-organs on the sideboard. Uncle Horatio—a thick-set, alert young man—would be standing at the organ, his broad fair-skinned face beaming as he turned from the music-sheets to greet me and adjusted the stool for me to sit down. I was very nervous and never made much headway with the lessons, but I liked the different atmosphere in Uncle Horatio. He had been converted at Trethosa chapel, and was the single wholesome exception in a family of raw pagans.

All this could be an allegory of my experience in 1956—the year in which I regained contact with the external world of music while visually imprisoned by the white scum. I was thankful that it was not a dark scum, for the psychological effects of white blindness are less damaging than those of the terrifying blackness which some blind people know. But what-ever form the blindness might take, I could not regard it in a simple practical way as a mere challenge to my courage and skill. I was writing a theological book and had to relate natural ills to ultimate questions of sin, guilt, punishment and expiation. These things might be dismissed as myths by most of my contemporaries, but even as myths they would have been more fascinating and important to me than the jargon of the welfare officers. The "ancestral mesh" was an indisputable fact: there was a dualism in which the marred body testified to the power of evil. My handicaps belonged to the world of my pagan forebears, not to that of pious Huguenots and Uncle Horatio. I was not sealed off for a life of quiet meditation, but more roughly reminded of the storm of human delinquency—the gutter and the guttering candle, the curses and sniggers on the stairs. How could anyone suppose that blindness would make me more of an idealist? It could bring me no vision of God, only a close-up view of the "Hogarth-smirch . . . the humped will in the twilight", as I put it in "The Veiled Sitter".

Even outside my own personal confrontation I was still in touch with the violence and horror which human instincts could produce. One of the first bits of news conveyed to me by my mother's palm-writing after I went blind was that there had been a murder at St Stephen's. An old widow called Whitford, who had sometimes poured out her troubles to my mother on the way home from Trethosa chapel, had been battered and strangled by her mentally defective son, with whom she lived alone in a bungalow. This was in the first week of 1956, and the sombre drama kept me realistic, partly distracting me from my own plight and even arousing gratitude as I contrasted the unhappy tensions of the Whitfords' home with the unity of faith and purpose between me and my mother. We knew how desperate my situation had become, and the burden was worse for Mother because she had heard that T was to be married at Easter—a fact I did not learn until several months after the wedding. There were moments when the tortured questionings of Job were wrung from us, but always in the context of the Christian death-and-resurrection pattern which saved us from despair. I saw that in my spiritual odyssey I had now reached the stage which most strongly counteracted the despondency a forty-year-old bachelor might feel at finding himself blind and deaf, living on a weekly Blind Persons' Assistance dole except for occasional small cheques from magazines and the BBC.

I had moved from a brooding isolationist worship to a quiet and reverent Anglican tradition, and from that to a buoyant and breezy revivalism. Now at the darkest hour this stimulus attained an exhilarating crescendo. My thoughts were abruptly switched from the St Stephen's murder and the foul slum stairs by the news that the teenaged American evangelist Renee Martz had started a campaign in Britain. My mother copied on my palm some newspaper reports of the meetings. Such activities might seem to be too trite and banal to impress a stern Kierkegaardian martyr, but the exuberance of this hot-gospel Pippa was to have repercussions in my life and work and inspire my next batch of religious poems. The Pippa element drew me back from nightmare into Browning's world, the world in which I could write *The Invading Gospel*. I had lost touch with it in my first dismay at going blind, but as I caught the young vibrant atmosphere of faith, the sense of "fellowship with the unwounded" (as I put it in "Prairie Song"), I was able to resume work on the book, scribbling the unseen letters from habit and memory, using a strip of cardboard to keep the lines straight. Here was further proof that although I might be inspired by "flashes struck from midnights" I could not be inspired by midnights. I was convinced that joy is the divine and human norm, that there is a fundamental unreality in all suffering which is not voluntary and vicarious (and therefore rooted in joy), and a consequent unreality and morbidity in the "lessons" we think we learn from it. The maps we draw amid the mists of sorrow are seen to be false guides when sunshine reveals the undistorted landscape.

I had not advanced many weeks into 1956 before it became evident that this was to be a year of new contacts and expansions, especially in the area of publicity. It was the year in which I first sat for portraits, and the year in which I first appeared on television. D. S. Savage had come up from Mevagissey with an artist friend of his, Lionel Miskin, who was very keen on my books and wished to put his own interpretation of me on canvas. He was just over thirty, an arresting and unusual figure—very tall and lean, with long sandy brown hair and beard: dressed like a tramp, a mixture of Bohemian and Franciscan, for he was a Roman Catholic. He had been born in France of privileged and cultured stock, and educated at

Oxford, but was now living a simple life of vehement protest against bourgeois security. He soon began writing on my palm, and we had some scrappy but interesting conversations. In February he made a drawing of me, and a little later I sat for a full-scale painting which was bought by Plymouth Art Gallery. It was not a flattering portrait, but it did suggest the soul of a persecuted Huguenot striving to become articulate through a deformed and stunted body—a symbol of the perverse twists in my family background. Lionel, of course, knew nothing about sixteenth-century French Clements; he depicted the character he had found in my early writings. His subsequent paintings of me were more attractive, particularly the one that was reproduced as a frontispiece in *The Map of Clay*.

Miskin loved the stark clay district and was already familiar with its southern fringe, as he taught art at a St Austell school. After visiting me he often came up to the hill country in his modest little car and, sitting on his stool in all kinds of weather, captured the unique angles and contours with his brush in a Van Gogh-like riot of colour. When he was painting landscapes near Goonamarris he would drop in at our cottage and have long talks with my mother. She welcomed his warm, eager approach, though she was sometimes shocked by his opinions. He was a Catholic humanist and tended to champion social misfits and rebels of every sort, including drug addicts and Beatniks. He seemed to regard Christ as an Angry Young Man, though he then accepted the orthodox doctrine of the Incarnation. While he and Mother chatted or argued I would slump a few feet away in my silent white world, in the fixed pallor that was not the whiteness of clay but of a ghostly No Man's Land, a battlefield from which the combatants had long since departed. Now and then some yellow or brown blobs would float across the white surface and fade at the corner of the eye, which still retained a glimmer of sight. I would watch these clouds or bubbles, knowing that I ought to see, instead of them, Lionel's thin arms waving and my mother's slow heavy figure leaning forward as she explained or refuted some point in the discussion. My mind was often working on *The Invading Gospel*—

thinking out new paragraphs, memorising paragraphs already written on the same subject, linking the fragments into coherent sections which I could dictate to Mother, who had begun writing passages of the book in longhand. At times I would become oblivious of the visitor until a gentle tap indicated that he wished to communicate some remark or question to me.

Lionel was the only male friend of mine who showed ease and confidence in palm-writing. The others either failed to make their markings intelligible to me or they were too sensitive to try. Charles Causley was in the latter group. He arrived at Goonamarris with Miskin one day during this period, and then with a BBC producer who had agreed to his suggestion that a film about me and the clay-pits should be included in a new television series. I had become familiar with Causley's breezy and explosive personality through corresponding with him, chiefly about broadcasts, since 1952, when I dropped him a handwritten note of thanks on finding his "Homage to Jack Clemo" in the *West Country Magazine*. I contributed to the same issue a minor poem in which I repudiated my Cornish clay world in favour of "Bulbarrow's brow" and the "wood-fanned Stour", and therefore apparently deserved the fate which Charles predicted for me:

> "Turn, Cornwall, turn and tear him,
> Stamp him in the sod. . . ."

Causley had sent me his early book of poems, *Farewell, Aggie Weston*, and I was relieved to discover that he was standing firmly on his own feet as a subtly allusive and lyrical sailor-poet. It was clear that there was no sign of a "school" of Cornish poets, all solemnly resolved to convey an identical Celtic faith or aura. The few modern poets who were born in the duchy had been too strongly moulded by non-Cornish influences— Causley by his naval experience, Rowse by Oxford, I by "foreign" writers and preachers and, since 1950, by the haunting otherness of Dorset. There might be Celtic fire in our imagination, but it warmed and illuminated totally different worlds of thought, motive and spiritual temper.

The whole household at Goonamarris, including Frances, found Causley's exuberance and spontaneity attractive. He was tall for a Cornishman (we are supposed to be short like the Welsh), and while his spectacles and schoolboyish quips denoted the teacher, there was a broader independence and loneliness in the blend of poet and sailor, his deeper self. Outwardly he looked neat, comfortable and well-groomed, with no trace of the rebellion against sleek society that was so obvious in Lionel and to some extent in me. On his first visit with the producer, having fixed a June date for the filming, he left the cottage with the jocular appeal to my mother: "Don't go running off to the South of France!" Actually, neither Mother nor I were likely to get stage-fright. We did not crave personal publicity, but as Mother so often said, "We must let our light shine," and we had no qualms about letting it flash on the television screen. My only regret was that the film unit hadn't come to Goonamarris before I went blind. The audience would now see me in a condition which would seem to justify the Helen Keller parallel, yet the poems read in the programme were written while my sight was good. Anyway, the weather was clear and brilliant when Causley reappeared with the technicians, and everyone seemed pleased with my performance. I did not feel nervous or embarrassed, but carried out the instructions as part of what I had been born for: walking unaided up the lane to the Slip, sitting among bushes on top of Bloomdale clay-dump. I did not speak in this film, which was devoted mainly to Causley's account of my life and background. Many viewers were impressed by it, though it did tend to suggest that I was on the screen chiefly because I had "overcome handicaps" and because I lived in a weird industrial area which offered splendid camera-material.

As the summer advanced, the early chapters of *The Invading Gospel* were completed in my mother's handwriting. I spent whole afternoons dictating to her. It was a severe strain on my memory, for I had to dictate passages I had scrawled three years before and hadn't seen for two years. Mother copied on my palm as much of the relevant fragments as she could decipher. She also spent hours wearily searching the pages of Browning, Barth, Lawrence and other writers to make sure my quotations were accurate. I could not have endured the frustration if I had not felt linked with a forward sweep of evangelism. Mother had kept me in touch with the Renee Martz campaign, and we had got as close to its atmosphere as we could by attending a Pentecostal healing service in a Plymouth mission-hall. It was very crude, and Mother said that most of the congregation were poor, shabbily-dressed slum-dwellers who yelled hymns out of tune or stamped about babbling in "tongues". This was not a climate in which I could feel at home. Still, it was another facet of Christianity and I tried to be sympathetic. But when I learnt that Renee Martz had recorded some of her solos I longed to hear her blithe Pippa-carollings in contrast to the rather unwholesome cacophony of the Plymouth crowd. I prayed about the matter and felt strangely challenged. By the end of August I had decided on what seemed to be one of my silliest ventures of faith. I would buy a record-player (we had got rid of our old worn-out gramophone soon after the war) and the Martz record, and somehow Providence would enable me to hear it. I had been almost stone deaf for several years, and specialists held out no hope that even a slight improvement was possible. But in cool disregard of this verdict I paid £14 for a second-hand record-player, and Mother brought home the record from a St Austell music shop.

For two months I played the record frequently without hearing a sound, and then one day in November, when I had a cold, I blew my nose and felt a squelching sensation deep inside my ear—and I heard myself cough. I hurried to fetch Renee Martz's record, and a few minutes later stood spell-bound, listening to her clear strong voice soaring amid a thunder of jazz. I could not catch any words, but the sounds were loud and incredibly moving after the years of silence. I had soon begun to shape the poem "Lunar Pentecost" to express the emotions that surged through me in those moments:

"A fire-flake has pierced my silence,
    And a tongue responds—too deep
To be greyly solemn, too sure
    Of heaven's glowing heart to let me sleep
With the sufferer's image, that cold fang
    Of lunar mystery. . . ."

I was back in aural contact with the external world, and have remained so ever since, except for brief relapses during illness. When a hearing-aid was issued to me I was able to pick up the usual sounds around the house, hear the kettle singing, the clock striking, Mother and Frances talking, but as I lacked co-ordination there was no trace of words from the human voices. It is impossible to say whether a more complete recovery would have changed my marriage prospects or my work.

At Easter 1957 there came a slight romantic tremor which is worth mentioning because it inspired a poem—"Modelled in Passion Week"—that may need a biographical key. Ernest Martin had turned up unexpectedly at Goonamarris with a London sculptress called Patricia who was staying with friends of his in Devon. She was a serious, heavily-built young woman in her early twenties, an Anglican, studying at the Royal College of Arts, where she had met Epstein. She was moved and fascinated when Martin told her about me, and after reading *Wilding Graft* she had felt urged to cancel her holiday plans and devote the entire Easter week to modelling a head of me in my home. I was very surprised when this news was broken to me. I realised that a whole week of sittings would be something of a strain, but I had been neglected by young ladies for so long that my male pride was flattered by the thought of a girl's eyes probing every detail of my face for hours each day, seeking to penetrate to my essential character. I agreed to the project, Patricia booked lodgings at St Austell and began coming out to Goonamarris on the early-morning bus, carrying her materials and tools. I wished I could see her at work. I sat relaxed and unmoving where she put me to get the best blend of light and shade, and tried to picture her studying my features from all angles and reproducing them with her skilled fingers in the modelling clay. She said she regarded the task as an offering to God and was praying that He would inspire her.

On the day of the first sitting she took back to her lodgings the two collections of my poems, and as she read them she grew aware that what she had to interpret was the soul of a man who believed that he was destined to marry. This seemed to arouse in her the same sort of religious and emotional questionings as Eileen and T had known. She was more mature, less impulsive than they, but when my mother told her how my hopes about them had been raised and dashed she admitted that she was wondering whether God had guided her to our cottage for a higher purpose than merely to produce a sculpture. . . . The situation was made more difficult by my inability to decipher much that she wrote on my palm. One morning she arrived while my mother was at the Post Office, and for half-an-hour Patricia and I were alone together in the house, but she gave no hint, in word or gesture, of any romantic inclinations. I was more exhausted by the last few sittings, feeling that we had made no headway at all in our relationship. On Good Friday she went to the Trethosa chapel service with Mother while I stayed at home and played the Renee Martz record.

When Patricia returned to London we tried to correspond, but there was a deadness, a failure to make contact. She knew that only my mother would read her messages and put my replies on paper, and this inhibited and embarrassed her. She sent us the finished head, cast in bronze plaster—a remarkable and generous gift which was exhibited at Truro Art Gallery later in the year. But her letters were stiff and impersonal, vaguely discussing aesthetic and religious values, and soon after Whitsun she penned a final note, assuring me of her prayers but stating: "I am quite unable to comprehend your feelings." There was an obvious split between the artist and the woman.

The artist in her had comprehended my feelings and breathed them into the sculpture. On first seeing the plaster cast Lionel Miskin exclaimed: "Why, it's full of passion!" As a creative artist she had been passionately interested in my physical appearance, finding clues to my personality in the rugged features—even in the saddle nose which had once led a visitor to say I looked like a boxer. Her intuitive powers had fused with the image, accepting and understanding it in the heat of inspiration. But when the image was fixed in clay and the creative fire died out, nothing was left except the sophisticated middle-class woman, the dignified Anglican who could not comprehend the raw village poet with his naïve enthusiasm for Yankee hot-gospellers. I could see what had happened in Patricia, and as there had been no word or touch of tenderness between us I was not much hurt by the abrupt end of our acquaintance.

A few days after I received Patricia's last note the BBC accepted "Lunar Pentecost" for a Sunday-morning religious broadcast, and I considered this to be adequate compensation for the disappointment. The proof that my revivalist phase had significance for the public spurred me on with the dictation of *The Invading Gospel*, and by September the book was finished. I found a pleasant irony in the fact that Patricia's friend, with whom she had stayed in Devon, had offered to type the book, and so my mother's manuscript with its weird spelling was posted off to a house near Beaworthy. It was copied in flawless typing in the room where Patricia had planned her Easter modelling of the strange poet in his remote white prison.

CHAPTER TEN

DUSKY INVASIONS

THE PATTERN OF the extraordinary, which has been so persistent throughout my life, is partly an inheritance. It was apparent at Goonvean Farm in the circumstances of my mother's birth and background. She was the last of twelve children, a very late arrival, her mother being forty-five and her father fifty when she was born. She knew her parents only as white-haired elderly people who had struggled through the ups and downs of married life for a quarter of a century, and buried six of their offspring, before they produced her. One of her brothers emigrated to America, and found a wife there, while Eveline was still a young child. Her sisters on the farm were eight or ten years older than herself, except the pathetic freak Bertha, three years her senior. The farm stood in the middle of the clayworks, which meant that when she played outdoors or went for a walk she was often watched by a dozen rough, swearing, hard-drinking labourers whose faces and voices frightened her. As the atmosphere of the home was intensely pious, her cheerful old father conducting family prayers every day as he knelt in front of the ragged arm-chair in the parlour, Eveline grew up making piety a protection against the feeling that she was somehow apart, inferior and insecure. She developed a solitary inner life of meditation and almost mystical awareness of the unseen, and was only super-ficially touched by the secular routine at Trethosa school.

Then at the age of fifteen her natural hunger fastened incon-gruously and desperately on the pagan extrovert, Reginald Clemo, who sang hymns with her in the chapel choir but had no spiritual interest in what the chapel stood for. Good-looking and vivacious, he fascinated her as they walked home together in the moonlight, following a path which skirted the edge of Trethosa clay-pit and then dipped into a secluded marshy hollow before climbing steeply to join a cart-track near Goonvean Farm. They were soon expressing a passionate and serious love, discussing domestic plans which led Reginald to emigrate to Montana, the copper mine belt where he could earn the high wages that would brighten their marriage prospects. At sixteen Eveline was wearing an American engagement ring while Reginald flirted with the exotic charmers in Butte saloons, perhaps regretting his weakness but helplessly drawn into the exciting swirl of the Wild West. He returned to Cornwall when his father died in 1912, and a year later Eveline married him, still wrapped in her religious dreams. The consequent disillusionment was bitter, and it was only in the long and lonely decades of widowhood that she gradually adjusted herself to a balanced and normal perspective.

I had never lived alone with my mother. The daily presence of the deformed Bertha may have inhibited us both; at any rate, when Bertha was absent for a few hours we often seemed to be a little strained and uneasy, shrinking from a heart-to-heart talk about our deeper human emotions. As we entered 1958 we realised that we would soon be an isolated couple in the house, for by this time Frances was engaged to a tall, sensitive young man called Raymond Brown whom she had met while working at Woolworth's stores at Newquay. We were relieved for Frances' sake, but we did not like the prospect of sharing the cottage without a third person to ease the abnormal pressures and help in an emergency. With Frances gone, I would be entirely dependent on my mother, not only for the typing of my letters and poems, but for the material—local gossip, newspaper reports, book reviews—that might give me something to write about, or at least think about, until I got involved in my next romantic venture. I was not the sort of mystic who could create poems which came exclusively from within his own soul, describing its communion with God in the manner of George Herbert and the hymn-writers. I was a spirit-and-sense mystic, and the artist in me demanded realism —landscapes, people, events. I had an inner vision that gave transcendent meaning to the external world, not an inner vision that was independent of the external world. And as there was a wayward, often an erotic element in both the vision and the realism, I chafed at the thought of entering a phase in which no one but my mother would be associated with the production of my work. Though Frances had not inspired me, she had kept the atmosphere of the house warm and vibrant with the pulse of young womanhood.

My mother was willing to make any effort or sacrifice to feed my sealed-off mind, but she was already disconcerted by the results. What she had told me about the Renee Martz campaign had led me to express, in poetry and prose, a view of Christianity as "God's jazz" or "Christ's ragtime sacrament" which seemed to her to be inconsistent with the awe and sense of divine chastening that an afflicted man should feel. She was grateful for the improvement of my hearing, but she attributed it to the earnest and, in her case, anguished prayers of Christians who expected my work to be a stern challenge wrung from the depths of suffering. She knew that I had plumbed such depths. She recalled me as a boy of five struggling and screaming in hysteria on the sofa as she approached me to put in the eye drops, my frantic resistance forcing her to strap me in a wheel-chair and take me to the doctor's surgery every evening for months. This first ordeal of semi-blindness had produced a fear-complex that crippled me for twenty years. Even in my thirties Mother had seen me in tears when Eileen and T dropped me, and when after straining for fifteen minutes to read a line of print, holding it at every possible angle to the light, I had to give up in defeat. Yet in my early forties my faith seemed to have become a bubble rather than a rock—or, more precisely, a paradoxical insistence that bubbles are the only rocks which can survive the sledgehammer blows of fate. I was being defiant in a new way. Perhaps Mother felt that the brash and vulgar American manners which had spoilt my father were now spoiling me—though I wrote "Prairie Song" to show that the two influences were poles apart.

I doubt whether my mother deliberately intended to correct my jazz capers when, in February 1958, she copied on my palm a lot of newspaper comment on the centenary of the Lourdes visions. She may have remembered that Helena Charles had seen me as a male Bernadette. I then knew little about the girl, but visionary experiences always made a strong appeal to me. I found myself comparing the Lourdes apparitions of Our Lady which led to the grey convent shadows, with Renee Martz's vision of Christ on the Los Angeles sidewalk, which led to flamboyant hot-gospelling. It took me four months to compose the poem "Beyond Lourdes", in which I contrasted the two types of vision and identified myself with the Evangelical, but also showed an understanding of the insights born of spiritual agony. When John Lehmann accepted the poem for the *London Magazine* he described it as "very strange and frightening". The jazz breaks in on the far side of nightmare, even though

"A soul unscarred
By mystic snow and border stream
May flash the healthier vision, spangled and starred."

Before this poem was finished, Mother and I were thrilled by Geoffrey Bles' acceptance of *The Invading Gospel*. I was back again as an English author after seven years' silence—and with a marked change of tone and style. This confirmed my belief that it was no cheap escapism which had led me to stress the bubbly joy of faith instead of repeating the grim, harsh moods of self-hatred and nature-hatred. It was all bound up with the truth that C. S. Lewis had grasped: "You die and die and then you are beyond death." What lies beyond death is immensely exhilarating, not dull and solemn. I remembered that during a black period of my youth I had written in my diary: "I have a constant feeling that I am now *beyond* the end and it is too late even to die." The sounding of the resurrection drums in the dark patch of my early forties was the antithesis of that youthful despair. I was not cultivating the natural cheerfulness which is so common among the handicapped. There was a profound spiritual law at work. Even my mother and the welfare officers (who still kept an eye on me) admitted that that there must be something in those aspects of my faith which seemed irreverent or irrational to them. Five years earlier the welfare ladies had predicted that if I didn't learn Braille or crafts or the manual alphabet I would go mad. Instead of doing any of these things I had produced a book which prompted the *Daily Telegraph* to inform its readers that "Jack Clemo is a happy man".

But though I was now expressing the buoyant Browningesque philosophy which I had always known to be my true message, I still lacked the enjoyment of the Wimpole Street pattern. I was mature as a Christian, but not as a man who had glimpsed the "intimate landscape". Loneliness and emotional frustration often clouded me, and when I sat in Nanpean chapel at Frances' wedding in November 1958, a few weeks after *The Invading Gospel* was published, I felt a deprivation and urgency regarding the book's teaching about the "personal covenant"—the pact with God for a fulfilment that is practical newspaper stuff. I was waiting daily for a letter from some unusual girl or woman who applied this principle in the same way as I did, and who would find in my book a call of affinity. I was prepared for the rare and incredible situation, in line with my mother's engagement to an absent lover at sixteen.

The next move, however, struck both my mother and myself as a baffling irony. A most unusual letter did arrive early in 1959, but the consequent relationship kept me in the continuous presence of tragedy for two years. The writer was a young Arab woman called Rosina, a Lebanese immigrant, and she poured out her harrowing story. Soon after her marriage in Egypt she had suffered a mental breakdown which led her husband to be unfaithful. They were divorced and he was given custody of their son. Her brother brought her to England to get the best medical treatment, but while in hospital she had attempted suicide. Eventually she was released, found lodgings in a London convent and became employed as a typist. She was still haunted by tormenting memories and fears, and was almost breaking down again when she discovered *The Invading Gospel* in a library and clutched desperately at its optimistic assurances. She asked for my advice and help, and for the rest of 1959 our correspondence was the chief feature of my life. Mother was kept busy copying Rosina's long letters on my palm and typing my replies. The woman's letters were in good clear English, for she was highly educated, a linguist in four languages. She had composed French verse, and had probably been a maladjusted neurotic dreamer before her marriage.

Her moods swung violently up and down: pages of feverish elation and black gloom would reach me during the same week. Then came a new development. She told me of her psychiatrist's verdict that she needed the security of an English home and that her best hope of a cure lay in remarriage. She asked me frankly how she was to find a husband, and the question prompted fantastic discussions in my remote cottage. Mother strongly urged me to say nothing that might make Rosina consider me as a possible partner. How could I dream of marrying an Arab divorcee who was fighting off mental illness? I clarified my reactions by writing a minor poem, "Lebanese Harvest", which summed up the poignancy of our contact. She left the Roman Catholic Church and joined an Evangelical group, and I tried to keep the correspondence clear of personal issues, merely consoling and instructing her on religious and practical points. Such restraint was not always easy. There were moments when I felt that this homeless foreigner might be the only woman in England who would be willing to marry me. I could at least give her British nationality and remove her fear of being deported and locked up in an Egyptian madhouse. Her mind was brilliant when freed from negative emotions; she was a skilled typist and would be a great help to me in my work. Above all, she shared my fervid yet subtle Christian faith. The real snag was her marriage, the thought of her ex-husband and child walking along beside the Nile as I wrote to her.

In June 1960 Rosina travelled down to Torquay for a holiday, intending to visit Cornwall and see me, but she became so depressed at the boarding-house that she fled back to London in a day or two. I never met her, and her letters grew less frequent. Some of them were unbearably painful, describing her renewed struggle against suicidal mania. A few of her pathetic later letters were written in hospital, but for about ten years she sent me Christmas cards expressing love and gratitude to me and my mother. The whole episode was, in a way, a check to my exuberance, reminding me that the mystery of human suffering cannot be glibly answered, and that there is no cure-all in religion or science, or in copulation and parenthood.

There was another reason why the year 1959 was rather subdued and shadowed at Goonamarris. I had finished a small collection of poems, *Frontier Signals*, but several publishers had refused it. When Charles Causley arrived one day with Colin MacInnes, my mother told them about my difficulties, and MacInnes—a tall serious man—generously offered to try to place the manuscript for me, as my former agent had lost interest in my work. At intervals during 1959 sad notes from Colin accompanied or soon followed desperate letters from Rosina. Publishers were still declining the little sheaf of poems I had written while my sight was slowly clouding over. It was not until January 1960 that MacInnes persuaded Methuen to take these poems as part of a collection which would include reprints of *The Clay Verge* and *The Wintry Priesthood*. Charles Causley suggested that a phrase from his poem on me could be used as a title for the volume, and throughout 1960 Rosina's letters were balanced by more cheerful ones about the forthcoming publication of *The Map of Clay*. MacInnes worked hard at building up support for the book, interviewing editors, reviewers and broadcasters. In November a television party came down from London and spent two days filming me and Mother and the clay-pits. For the indoor shots my mother had to bring tea to my desk from the kitchen, and unfortunately she tripped over a rug and fell heavily, breaking a rib against the arm-chair. She was in severe pain next morning, but insisted on completing the film before she called in a doctor and had the bone set. She was resting in bed at Christmas when I handed her the fifty-guineas cheque we had just received from the television company. The payment bewildered her: "We didn't do nothing but walk around," she said.

Charles Causley drove across Bodmin Moor to visit us fairly often during this period. Once he arrived with a Roman Catholic priest, once with a college tutor who wrote an article about me (printed in a magazine for the blind), and once with the American poet Daniel Hoffman and his wife and children. Hoffman was very keen on my books, and published in the *Transatlantic Review* a poem reflecting his reactions to my life and environment. Only on one occasion did Causley come to my home alone, and that was when he wanted to discuss with Mother the preface he had agreed to write for *The Map of Clay*. I was, of course, an awkward subject for a confirmed bachelor to interpret. Nearly all my writings had flowed from emotional attachments which I dramatised as Wimpole Street romances. For twenty-five years I had been sustained and vitalised by the belief that God had destined me for marriage, and that for this very reason the devil had tried to make me unmarriageable. This was implied in my themes and Mother had made it explicit to journalists and broadcasters. They seemed embarrassed, and chose to present me as an unromantic but courageous man who had triumphed over handicaps by writing books that were said to have merit. Causley took much the same line, and I knew that it was well-meant. My literary friends wished me to be admired as an artist, not ridiculed or pitied as an absurd sentimentalist who was consoling himself with fantasies about marriage. The whole truth about me could not be told unless and until I married. On this basis, Causley's preface was a skilful and sensitive appreciation.

I felt less sympathetic, however, regarding some of the reviews. *The Map of Clay* was given a wider press coverage than any of my other books, including feature notices in several national dailies. Kenneth Allsop, in a long review in the *Daily Mail*, described me as "the Bunyan of the clay-pits". I was pleased by the comparison, though it was an over-simplification, since Bunyan had never been guilty of erotic mysticism or jazz capers. He was a plain John Bull in religion and literature, while I was anything but a John Bull. I was blunt and forthright at so many different points that I ceased to be plain, or even intelligible, to those who could not grasp a complex vision. Few critics showed any awareness of the intricate weaving of my moods and ideas. But what really exasperated me was the flood of false statements about my private circumstances. Readers were told that I had been blind since I was five, that I lived in darkness and silence, that I was sunk in deepest poverty and had never stepped outside my little Cornish clay-patch. I shuddered to think of the effect these lies would have on a girl or woman who had been romantically stirred by my poems. My faith for marriage would have been strained by all this humiliating publicity had not a sudden turn in February 1961 made the practical foundation of that faith stronger than it had ever been before.

It was the result of action taken by Derek Parker, the Cornish broadcaster and journalist. He had first contacted me in 1956 when, as dramatic critic of the *Western Morning News*, he was writing an article on my poetry. Soon afterwards he married and settled in London, where he worked for the BBC. He and his vivacious wife, Julia, had called at my home several times while on holiday in Cornwall. He had discussed with Charles Causley the possibility of obtaining a Civil List pension for me. An attempt had been made in 1950 when my publishers sent an appeal to Attlee, signed by many eminent authors, including T. F. Powys, Aldous Huxley and Howard Spring. Attlee's advisers apparently thought me too young to be pensioned, but the appeal gave me a place in the Downing Street files, and when at the end of 1960 Derek Parker raised the question again, it was promptly and favourably considered. In February Harold Macmillan recommended me for an award, and just after the postman called at Goonamarris on the morning of Friday, 3 March, my mother slapped me on the back and then wrote excitedly on my palm: "Praise the Lord! You got nearly £5 a week pension from the Queen."

CHAPTER ELEVEN

A VALKYRIE IN LAKELAND

AFTER FRANCES MARRIED, my emotional life was at times in danger of slipping back to the level on which it functioned during the war. From 1958 to 1963 the only feminine stimulus I received (apart from the correspondence with Rosina) came from my cousin, Maria Wilcox, who had been born while I was in the glow of my Dorset visit in 1950. Each summer she travelled down from London with her mother or grandmother and spent a few weeks of her holiday at my cousin Viney's home on Carne Hill, St Dennis. She would come to our cottage for an occasional afternoon, and on three or four other days my Roche cousin Annie would take the whole family group to a beach—Porthpean, Caerhayes, Perranporth or Newquay. Maria would lead me out for a paddle, and I would be conscious only of her small hand holding mine and my feet treading dry sand, then moist sand, then the first ripples of the tide. I knew that Maria was wearing a bathing-suit, but I had no individual picture of her in my mind. I had never seen her, as she had been born in Wales and then moved to London and had not met me or my mother before I went blind. These beach diversions were refreshing, yet strangely unreal: the little hand reaching me out of a blank and leading me through a blank, with no face, no personality. Maria was more solid and complete to me at home, sitting on my knee and scrambling with me around Bloomdale clay-dump. We would return to the road through a defile overhung with brambles, and she would protect me from the trailing thorns. This inspired some lines of my poem "Bedrock":

"A playful hand lifts back the bramble
From my blind groping face."

I was repeating the old trick, dramatising childish contacts, making them serve my faith for a lover and wife. It was psychologically more satisfying because I was no longer the penniless, unknown struggler who had kissed Barbara and Irene. Maria was proud of her "famous cousin". She was thrilled to see me on television in London, and to find photographs of me in the *Sunday Times Colour Supplement* in 1962 when Derek Parker contributed a feature about me to this paper. But the episodes with Eileen, T and Patricia had pointed to mature fulfilment, and as I drifted into my middle forties I prayed for this more and more urgently. By the end of 1962 my mother realised that I could not stand the strain much longer. A fortnight before Christmas Frances' first child was born, and within a few hours Violet's husband took me and Mother to St Columb Minor, near Newquay, and I was led into the bedroom where Frances lay. The baby, a girl, was placed in my arms, and as I felt her gentle movements and the touch of the warm new-born skin, I knew I could find no "compensation" in a twelve-year-old cousin, and certainly not in the mental creativity of a bachelor poet. I was essentially domestic: the bounty of womanhood in the settled routine of home-life was infinitely more important to me than art.

I entered 1963 in spiritual storm, gripped by a sense of crisis and determined to reach a breakthrough. It came towards the end of January, and in the way I had been waiting for. A letter posted in a Devonshire coastal town plunged me into my first full-scale romance, which was to fill the next four years with all the joys and miseries of an incredibly unconventional attachment and give my poetry an altogether new slant. There were no formal or friendly preliminaries, only the headlong collision and ignition of two lonely social misfits.

The letter was from Mary, who introduced herself as an art teacher in her early thirties. She had been profoundly disturbed and haunted by my poems and autobiography, and she begged me not to confuse her letter with typical fan-mail. She was praying that her message would reach me safely, as she felt an overwhelming urge to visit me as soon as I fixed a convenient week-end. I had never received a letter which carried such obvious emotional implications. I replied briefly, inviting her to spend the first week-end in February at my home. She answered more fully and warmly, enclosing a photograph of herself and asking Mother to describe it to me. She looked healthy and strongly built, with a dreamy mystical expression on her face, but also a force of character which we were later to call Scandinavian, the Valkyrie image. Her parents came from the north of England, and her heart was in the Lake District. She gave some details about her frustrated life and her attitudes, saying she was too religious to go to church, and that she found in my work the same vital truths which she admired in D. H. Lawrence. This statement troubled me; it revealed the bias that was to cause so much unhappy friction. She seemed to think that my vision was intrinsically pagan, and that I was giving it church labels to please my mother.

On the day of her arrival torrential rain poured over the clay area from dawn till dark. Mother and I hired a taxi and went to meet Mary at St Austell station at 9 am. Mary came towards us like one in a trance; she did not shake hands, but when I climbed into the taxi she stole quietly in beside me and took my hand caressingly in hers. It was a strange silent ride back to Goonamarris through the pounding wind and rain. When we got indoors Mary was soon sitting close to me and writing on my palm more clearly and rapidly than anyone else had done. We joked and talked about her Devon lodgings, not at all embarrassed by my handicaps. But as the day wore on the atmosphere grew tense and smouldering. She was a brilliant and vehement talker, and she told my mother bluntly that the religious narrowness of dogma and revivalism would choke and cripple me as an artist. She was going to get "really tough" with me and make me the natural, untrammelled erotic mystic I was meant to be. She loved my true self and would free it from the straitjacket of old-fashioned piety. Such aggressive frankness after only a few hours' acquaintance left my mother a bit dazed, and when Mary caught the bus at Nanpean on Sunday evening both of us in the cottage felt limp, as if a volcano had erupted in our midst. Mother thought it would be best for me to break off such a dangerous association before I was swept off my feet.

I wrote a rather cool note to Mary, but she replied with a passionate letter, protesting that we had misunderstood her. She was the same sort of elemental Christian as I was. She had written a thesis on Blake at college and shared his approach to Christianity. If it seemed to have pagan elements this was because the higher paganism contained the same truth as mystical non-church Christianity, and that was surely what we both wished to express in an erotic relationship. . . . I gave her the benefit of the doubt. She might be near the Kingdom, and perhaps I could help to draw her fully in. We continued to exchange love letters (I added intimate handwritten postscripts to the letters I dictated to my mother), Mary spent a further week-end at our home, and we decided to become informally engaged at Easter when she would stay at Goonamarris for a whole fortnight. I bought an illustrated Bible as my betrothal present to her, and she had a pair of photographs of herself and us enlarged and framed as her betrothal gift to me.

The Easter fortnight was a mixture of bliss and uneasiness. Every morning I took breakfast upstairs to Mary and sat on the bed while she drank her tea. We had long discussions alone there until my mother suddenly opened the door and handed me the mail, which Mary would copy on my palm. In the afternoons we went out for walks around Trethosa or Carloggas, and on Easter Sunday we attended the christening of Frances' baby, Mandy, at Nanpean chapel. I wanted Mary to see the unusual features I had written about, so I asked Mother to lead us to the old water-wheel in Goonamarris copse—the subject of my poem "The Water-wheel" and the scene of Shirley's death in *Wilding Graft*. Much to our disappointment, we found that the wheel had been demolished since I went blind: nothing remained but the overgrown concrete base and a few stumps of rotting wood. Mary loathed the clay-tips as industrial scabs and could only accept them as "white elephants". She wished I could take her out to the coast like a normal lover. The nearest we got to this was when Lionel Miskin came up one day and drove us in his car along the coast road to Mevagissey. Mary enjoyed having tea with his petite long-haired wife, Pru, and their children. The small house had an aura of Bohemian zest and freedom which Mary approved of. We all went out for a stroll around the quaint little fishing village. In previous years Lionel had shared Helena Charles' view that I might function to the end as a lonely, suffering visionary, but when he saw me walking through the streets with a solid and sophisticated young woman on my arm, he changed his mind and felt that God had worked a more human miracle.

Yet there was, as I put it in my poem "The Leper", a knot in it. Mother was torn between gratitude and fear. She saw that Mary's love was "pulling me together" as a man while subtly threatening me as an orthodox believer. In practical matters she saw Mary succeeding where she herself had failed. Mary insisted that I must amend my personal habits—clean my teeth daily, take more baths (standing in a zinc bath in the kitchen), wear pyjamas (my autobiography had revealed that I slept in my shirt), and learn Braille and typing. From my new perspective as a lover it all seemed reasonable, and I complied. It was obvious that if at any time my mother were too ill to copy letters or type at my dictation, Mary and I would be unable to correspond unless I could type and we both learnt Braille. And so, in the spring of 1963, an astonished welfare officer was giving me weekly Braille lessons and I was counting the keys in each row of my typewriter, memorising their position and learning to tap the right key. In a month or two I was reading Braille books and typing my own letters and poems. There was a general sense of awakening and advance. A long radio feature on my life and work was broadcast twice in the BBC Third Programme. Mary heard it in her Devon lodgings and was very proud. Then Penguin Books asked me to select twenty of my poems for *Penguin Modern Poets 6*, and Mary helped me to compile the list, which included two poems about our attachment—"Confessional" and "The Leper".

But all this soon headed into cruel irony. During her Whitsun visit to my home Mary became more realistic about our domestic and social problems. The romantic novelty of loving a blind and deaf poet had worn off; she was increasingly irked by the restrictions my handicaps imposed. She had lived all her life among cultured middle-class people, and was now conscious of being repelled by my crude environment—even my mother's dialect. She had misgivings about our betrothal, and these were deepened at the start of the summer holidays, when she travelled to the Lake District with her mother and sister. They were hostile to the idea of her marrying me, and her mother put forward a counter-plan. She had been recently widowed, and she wished to retire to Westmorland with Mary living close by, working at a Lakeland school. The proposal gripped Mary as she felt again the enchantment of the lakes and mountains. Her commitment to me amid the mud and clay-pit noises of Goonamarris seemed unreal, a mistake. She applied for a teaching job almost on the shore of Windermere, and in August she came down to my cottage to break the stunning news that she could not continue our relationship. She had often wished to start a new life in the Lake District, which was her true home, and now the call was clear and irresistible. She was very upset, knowing what a devastating blow her decision would be to me and my mother, but the fresh contact with her family, the memories of her childhood raptures among the fells, had made her realise that she could never fit into my way of life. One afternoon while Mother was absent, Mary destroyed all the love letters she had sent me, and three days later she bade us farewell.

I was ill for several weeks, yet somehow I could not accept this as final, and on 12 September—the anniversary of Browning's marriage—I wrote her a brief note of enquiry. She replied at once, saying she was willing to keep in touch with me as a friend. We exchanged a few awkward, groping letters, but restraint was difficult and soon there were signs that our emotions were pressing forward again. "I only want to be with you, yet when I am with you I can't bear it," she confessed. In October we dropped all pretence and resumed the old tenderness, and in November we had an incredibly happy week-end of reconciliation before she left Devon for Westmorland. She had taken lodgings there, as her mother had not yet bought a house in the North. Our letters flowed faster than ever—two or three a week. I sent drafts of new poems for her judgement, and owed much to her candid criticism. She would pounce on a jerky rhythm, a stale adjective, or the general flatness of a line or stanza. She urged me to be more objective and stop writing "diary poems". She hadn't liked "The Leper", which I had shown her while she lived in Devon. "I want you to write poems *for* me, not *about* me," she explained. We worked together on my sonnet "Lines to Wordsworth", which she loved for its evocation of Lakeland. But she was anxious that I should cultivate a more modern style, so I began studying Eliot, Rilke, Hopkins and Dylan Thomas in Braille. The effect of this was first apparent in "Eros in Exile", a complex imagist presentation of natural sexuality in search of divine grace:

> "Foiled bud and wing, soiled catkins—and above, outside,
> Wooden beams crossed on the clay-hill.
> Another cry, a tie with another temple,
> More deeply penetrating:
> By the rivers of Babylon
> We lay down but could not love. . . ."

At Easter Mary made the long journey to Cornwall in order to build up our renewed betrothal. Its course was still beset by storms. My mother had lost confidence in Mary and the atmosphere was strained. Mary and I sometimes clashed on religious and moral issues, and her detestation of the clayworks became so intense that on returning to Westmorland she wrote bluntly: "I do want to marry you, Jack, but I *won't* live in Cornwall." I must visit the Lake District and see if I could settle there. This ultimatum forced a new crisis. My mother, now over seventy, was dismayed, dreading the thought of being uprooted, or of my being wrenched away from her. Yet she had to admit that Mary was giving me the help and comfort which the church girls had denied me, and so with a blind trust in Providence she agreed to spend a week with me at Mary's lodgings.

Mary travelled down to escort us on this first frightening journey to Windermere. I sat close to her in the carriage, awed and tense, feeling the August sunshine as the train roared northward along the Welsh border, and then, as nightfall approached, the cool sea breeze blowing in through the open window. We stepped into the corridor, and Mary told me we were skirting Morecambe Bay with the lights of Barrow twinkling across the estuary. Cornwall seemed very far away, small and faded beyond Lawrence's collieries and Bennett's Potteries, and I had to adapt myself to Mary's country without seeing it—just letting it flow into me through her touch. Mother and I were exhausted when at last we got into a taxi at Windermere station, but we felt better next day, and Mary took us for a walk around the edge of the lake to Adelaide's Hill, where we had our first taste of the vigorous, pelting Lakeland rain. On subsequent days we had bus rides to Keswick and Dungeon Ghyll. Mary wrote constantly on my palm, describing the scenery, the shapes of the mountains as they came in sight—Helvellyn, Scafell, Skiddaw, Glaramara. At Keswick I mused about Ruskin at Friar's Crag, enjoyed a launch trip with Mary on Derwentwater, and (less enjoyably) bumped my head against Hugh Walpole's tall tombstone. At Dungeon Ghyll Mary and I scrambled around the fissured base of Langdale and she put my hand on the delicate rowans and into a turbulent beck. I responded vividly and felt that if I were not blind I could live quite happily in this magnificent rugged region.

But the visit had a sorry close, with Mary expressing fresh

doubts about marrying me, and though I was under the impression that she was returning to Cornwall with us to spend a few days at Goonamarris, she got off the train at Crewe, and for the rest of the journey south I sat alone with Mother, bewildered and depressed. Mary's next letter, however, assured me that her love was unchanged, and I had soon written some sensitive and poignant poems about our Lakeland excursions. The autumn passed in quiet suspense. My Penguin poems were published and I sent a copy to Windermere. Frances had another baby, Margaret, and I felt how unbelievably my life had been transformed since Mandy was born. My family and Cornish friends were watching my strange romance with puzzled curiosity, speculating about Mary's motives. At Christmas my mother slipped on an icy road and broke her wrist a few days before Mary arrived, and as a result of this Mary was virtually running the house for a week. The shared domesticity drew us closer, and we entered 1965 in a mood of confidence, looking forward to my return to Westmorland in the spring. We had developed a habit of reading the same book simultaneously and discussing it—Mary her normal print copy, I a Braille one—in our letters and talks. Our study of Franz Werfel's *The Song of Bernadette* prompted me to write two poems on the Lourdes miracle—very different from "Beyond Lourdes", for in 1961 a Roman Catholic visitor had given me a phial of water from the Massabieille spring, and as I sprinkled the drops on my forehead at intervals since then I had been drawn into a great mystery and benediction. Mary and I both accepted Bernadette's vision as authentic: Mary loved the stark, simple, primitive experience of saints like St Francis and Bernadette, and for this very reason she detested the organised churches in which no one was allowed to see visions or look like a Beatnik.

My second visit to the Lake District in April was more satisfactory than the first. Its highlight was the pilgrimage to Grasmere, where we were conducted over Dove Cottage and I touched Wordsworth's arm-chair and his curtained bed, conscious of the irony (for I had been a violently anti-Wordsworthian poet), and then Mary had led me up the stony path behind the cottage. We sat on Wordsworth's garden seat and talked of his love for Annette Vallon and the later years when he had rested on this same seat with his wife and Dorothy, his emotions a veiled, twisted enigma. The day after our exploration of Grasmere we stood at Ruskin's grave in Coniston churchyard and spoke of his tragic passion for Rose La Touche: the spiritual split so like our own, Evangelical faith in one partner clashing with natural mysticism and scepticism in the other. There were still many shadows and uncertainties. I could not definitely promise to settle in Westmorland while blind, and my mother felt that the day-long journey taxed her strength too heavily for her to bring me up for a third Lakeland trial. In the summer Mary came to Cornwall for a week, then spent the remainder of her holiday in Scotland. While she was there I was disturbed and thrown back fourteen years by the news that a poignant domestic tragedy had befallen T. My confused reactions were expressed in "Summer Saga" with its hint that T's suffering might

> "Pierce the dried memory
>   Of her flight from this fluttering cone
>   When a summer's promise turned
>   To dust-swarms, maggots on the bone."

I was torn between past and present, filled with vague regrets; and from this time onward things did not go well in my relationship with Mary. Her Christmas visit began with the old ardour, but the uncongenial milieu, the pettiness of "little walks" when she wanted to spend a whole day climbing Scafell, and the pressure of my mother's piety and unease about us, soon made her tense and explosive; and though she came to Goonamarris again at Easter there were fresh wrangles and a feeling of disintegration. We continued to correspond, trying desperately to find some solution that would be at least tolerable to us all, but we could see none. In July she went to Scotland, and while in the Isle of Skye she reached a point where she could bear the fruitless inner conflict no longer. She decided not to visit me again. My poem "Harpoon" commemorates this decision. It was a heartbreaking end to our three-and-a-half years' "miracle romance". Mary tried to soften the blow by writing me occasional letters of tender understanding until December 1966. Then there was silence, and I could only finger a big pile of love letters which I had never read.

CHAPTER TWELVE

RUTH

BEFORE I RECEIVED Mary's final letter I had given my first television talk. Westward Television at Plymouth decided to make a long film about me at a rather awkward moment. When my mother was asked how I had developed since I went blind, she had to confess that my life and work had been completely changed through a romance with an art teacher. The producer wanted to broadcast some account of this romance and put photographs of Mary on the screen, but I had to bar such publicity, not only because the betrothal had been broken off, but also because Mary had often said that if she married me she would never consent to our appearing on television: it would be too humiliating, focusing attention on my handicaps and preventing viewers from taking me seriously as an artist. In my brief talk I mentioned my visits to the Lake District but not my romance, and ended by saying: "I don't know what my ulitmate landscape will be, but I'd prefer to settle in my own clay world." This simply meant that without being able to see a new environment I could not fully absorb it, even though it now suited me better than the industrial scabs around Goonamarris. I was in no danger of relapsing into my old hermit state. It was the lonely, starved, immature self which had found the gaunt and blasted clayworks its true home, and that self could never revive. I felt an unbearable poignancy of loss during the early months of 1967, but not the sort of loneliness I had known before Mary came. My heart was stored with a lover's memories. Her love letters still seemed to breathe a warm, vital pride around me. I still knew the time of day or night only through the embossed watch she had given me on my forty-eighth birthday.

My first practical task was to retype and arrange the poems which Mary had directly or indirectly inspired—nearly a score —and add the various other poems I had written since 1961, making a new collection entitled *Cactus on Carmel*. I was struck by its breadth of range: it opened in the Mexican desert and closed in St Thérèse's convent at Lisieux, and there was very little in it about Cornish clay-pits, with which so many critics had said I was obsessed. When the book was promptly accepted for publication later that year, I realised that Mary had not come into my life by chance or mistake, however baffling it might seem that an anti-church aesthete should mould and liberate a writer who was drawing nearer to the churches and loathed aestheticism. *Cactus on Carmel* was less Evangelical than *The Map of Clay*, and had a vein of Catholic mysticism which puzzled those who had labelled me "Calvinist". The Bernadette poems and "Cactus in Clayscape" showed a deep imaginative and spiritual sympathy with the Marian doctrines. I had discussed them with Mary, but she could not accept any Catholic dogmas and regarded my poems about them as mere speculative works of art. To me they were something more than that. I was not just an artist presenting the devotional life of French nuns. I was an explorer of Christianity, and having proved that bubbly revivalism was as valid as stern Calvinism I now felt that at least some Roman Catholic emphases might be as valid as Protestant ones. The Immaculate Conception and the Assumption were not essential to my theological pattern, but when I used Lourdes water I was convinced that its implications were within the revelation of divine grace, not outside in the realm of natural mythology. My Catholic poems had special significance in relation to Mary's shaping of my work. In writing the erotic and Lakeland poems I owed every-thing to her, but when I wrote of the Virgin or stated that an ecstatic nun is superior to a materialistic wife (as I did in "Carmel"), I was following my own independent line of development, whether Mary approved of it or not.

Apart from the satisfaction of having my new book in the press, I was confused and fretted throughout the summer of 1967. Some of my friends, distressed by my inability to get out and make fresh contacts, offered to try to discover a pen-friend, preferably a spinster, who might ease the strain. As a result of this I received a few stiff and hesitant letters from a Quaker lady, but the contrast with Mary's brilliant, passionate out-pourings was too painful and I could not go on. The Methodist minister who had succeeded Gordon Turner at St Dennis and had met Mary several times, had now left Cornwall, but on learning of my plight he asked the young people's group at Nanpean chapel to visit me occasionally. He thought the presence of lively young Christians in the house, talking to me in palm-writing, perhaps singing choruses that I could hear faintly, would help to keep me from stagnant brooding. My mother had told me about one of the girls in this group—a radiantly religious college student called Sylvia Crowle who was very keen on my poetry and sometimes recited it at chapel concerts. It would have given me a vaguely authentic pleasure to meet Sylvia, and I waited hopefully during vacations; but she did not come, and in December I was shocked and sincerely grieved by the news that she had been killed in a car crash while returning home from Oxford. I wrote the poem "A Nanpean Student" in tribute to her.

Before I composed my poignant yet triumphant stanzas on Sylvia's death, I was treasuring more love letters—and this time there was to be no slip or breakdown. I had reached the end of my long odyssey of faith and was in the warm, trust-worthy currents around the harbour. There was a constant pulse from the scenes which had been charged with the sense of a benevolent destiny eighteen years earlier—my enchanted Dorset. I knew now that while I stood on Bulbarrow on that August day in 1950, looking towards the coast with my slightly blurred eyes, a girl in her middle twenties was struggling with the effects of a deep emotional wound as she packed linen at the South Dorset Laundry in Weymouth. She was Ruth Peaty —a tall, slender young woman with a delicate oval face, long brown hair held loosely around her head by clips, and blue eyes which had a naturally vivacious sparkle but also showed pain and a momentary flash of rebellion when she lapsed into silent questioning. For the most part she joined in the chatter of the other work-girls, sometimes laughing and revealing her white irregular teeth, but the bruised spirit in her longed to get away alone in her favourite haunt—the Old Castle Gardens on Weymouth cliffs—where she could contemplate the palms and the quiet sea caressing the green finger of Portland, and commune with the ultimate love that made her feel the intact dedication of a nun. She was in no mood to accept a Cornish lover when I went to Dorset.

Ruth's first letter to me was dated 12 September, and I noted the coincidence—the date of Browning's wedding anniversary again. She wrote to me because a friend had told her about my books and she wanted further details; she also felt that I must be "an interesting person". I sent her a copy of *The Invading Gospel*, and its odd mixture of autobiography, polemics, evangelism, poetry and literary criticism seemed to meet her need of a more complex approach than that of the average religious book. Her subsequent letters were thoughtful and sharply honest, and we soon discovered that we had remarkable affinities in background and vision. She had been born in London, but her father, William Peaty, was a Dorset man, a native of Poole. Like my father, he had joined the Navy, but had been psychologically damaged by the horrors of battle and, being a devout member of the Plymouth Brethren, had prayed desperately for a wife whose love would help his recovery. On returning to London he had met a young widow, Mabel Rhodes, who was training for missionary work in India. After some hesitation she became convinced that God willed her to stay in England, that her vocation was to heal and liberate this impoverished and stricken marine from Poole. They married with little money and no worldly prospects, in simple faith that God had ordered their union. They had five children and struggled through many dark patches, including the loss of two of their infant sons. William Peaty never fully recovered from the war-shock, but he took part in evangelistic tours and for a short period held a job as a relief officer. He died when Ruth was twelve, and five years later, during the blitz, she was evacuated to Weymouth with her mother and younger sister Bella.

In spite of the hardship and tragedy of her childhood, Ruth was a healthy and high-spirited teenager, very attractive to boys. But they found her elusive and mystifying: her surface gaiety and impish teasing were combined with strict Christian morals, and later, under the influence of a dynamic visionary friend, an unmarried lady from Torquay, a few years her senior, she developed a rare spiritual approach to love, sex and marriage. She didn't want simple desire and pleasure, but something beyond instinct. When she got engaged it was to a marine who was also a member of the Brethren and filled his love letters with texts from the Bible. As the months passed, however, he began to doubt whether their marriage was "the Lord's will", and after nearly eight years of suspense in which they lived like a monk and nun and only prayed for each other, he married someone else. Ruth was crushed and bitterly dis-illusioned, and during the years of waiting she suffered a further cruel blow. Her once brilliant brother Jacob (called "Jack" by his family) showed increasing signs of schizophrenia and was spending his adult life in hospital.

Ruth sought consolation in a more intense religious ex-perience, eagerly absorbing the Biblical and devotional teach-ing of the Torquay visionary, who acted as a sort of Mother Superior to her during her ascetic phase. Then gradually the extreme reaction gave place to a more balanced outlook. The Billy Graham films and crusades helped to free her from sectarian bias. In 1954 she travelled to London with a mixed crowd of young church people and heard Graham preach at Harringay. She had her hair cut short, wore trousers, and read widely in secular literature. Up to the time she first heard of me she had avoided fresh emotional involvements, and had refused the overtures of one or two religious men. She would probably have been content to accept me as a pen-friend, but when I told her about Mary and sent her *Cactus on Carmel*, explaining what it felt like to be jilted at fifty, she was sorry for me and the woman in her aroused and challenged. By Christmas 1967 we were discussing the possibility of our marriage, and early in 1968 our letters became tender and caressing. This did not come easily to me; I was still to some extent under Mary's spell, and Ruth showed deep understanding of my difficulties. We longed to meet, but Ruth could not get a week's holiday until June, and so our romance was, on the physical level, a sharp contrast to my relationship with Mary. All I knew of Ruth came through my mother's finger moving patiently on my palm.

I was often alone in the house while typing my letters, for at this period my mother was attempting to help a tragic old lady who lived by herself in a nearby bungalow. A widow and almost friendless, this semi-literate village woman had grown senile and was afflicted with delusions. Sometimes she came banging on our door after dark, very distressed and agitated, and told Mother that her own mother's ghost was in the bungalow, sitting at the table or waiting on the stairs, and that she was frightened. On one such occasion Mother and I went back to the bungalow with her to dispel her fears. Mother did what she could for the woman, spending an hour or two with her in the afternoons. I was troubled about the situation when I thought of asking Ruth to settle at our cottage. At best it could hardly be charming or desirable to one who had lived for twenty-five years in a beautiful suburb of Weymouth. The clayworks were still spreading scars around the grim, damp little house. The Nanpean-St Stephen's road, which passed directly outside our garden wall, was being closed, and a field had been torn to pieces to make room for an alternative route a hundred yards farther down the hill. How would Ruth react if, in addition to this ugliness, the poor terrified old woman came rushing to our home, gabbling wildly about ghosts? But I need not have worried, as the woman was taken ill and removed to hospital, where she died before Ruth slept under the grey slates at Goonamarris.

The midsummer day of our first meeting arrived at last. Ruth and her sister Bella—who was also single and worked as an accountant in a Weymouth office—had booked a room at a Porthpean guest-house, and on the afternoon of Sunday, 23 June, my mother and I set out for Nanpean to meet them as they walked down past Drinnick wharf from the bus-stop. We both felt pretty sure that on this warm, quiet afternoon I would encounter my future wife. I was inwardly warm and quiet myself, trustful and curious but not excited. I hadn't even seen Ruth's photograph, so there was as yet no appeal to the senses. Our discussions about marriage had been based on faith and the affinities of personality we saw in each other's writings. I had not written any poems on Ruth, though I sometimes sent her light-hearted and humorous verse to relieve the seriousness of our reflections and disclosures about religion and family tragedy. I knew that I was going to contact a most unusual character, with a touch of the nun still restraining the childlike, headlong impulses that kept her a potential rebel. I knew that her mind was full of questions about the meaning of life and dissatisfied with the glibly orthodox answers, yet aware that un-orthodox answers were even less satisfying—that the humanist answers were absurd over-simplifications and the popular mystical answers mere drugs. The Quaker lady had put me off at the start by praising the enlightened Bishop of Woolwich and his honest-to-Robinson mythology, but as my mother led me towards Nanpean on this June Sunday I was cheered by the knowledge that Ruth preferred *The Invading Gospel*.

We had almost drawn level with the huge electrical power station at Drinnick when Mother glimpsed the two colourful figures approaching—Ruth slim and girlish, Bella more solid, with a round pleasant face and glasses. I shook hands with them and walked back to Goonamarris beside Ruth, scarcely speaking a word, conscious that I had begun one of the most momentous weeks of my life. At the cottage I soon realised that Ruth's "atmosphere" was magnetic, but she flicked her finger nervously across my palm in a way that failed to make the words clear to me. We had to get through a major problem in "situation ethics". How could we develop our attachment without conversation? Obviously the neat formulas of normal friendship and courtship must be abandoned. A blind and deaf man cannot play the traditional masculine rôle; he cannot be the hunter, for he cannot even know that the beloved is in the room with him unless she takes the initiative and touches him. . . . In the evening we all went to Trethosa chapel and I prayed in my old pew, feeling Ruth's arm move restlessly against mine. The spiritual tide rose and conventional rules ceased to matter. The signal was given, and I kissed Ruth good-night as she left our cottage to catch the return bus.

Next day we were still baulked in our attempts to converse, and Ruth went back to Porthpean depressed and doubtful. She prayed long and earnestly at the guest-house, and on the Tuesday she arrived at Goonamarris in a more confident mood and started writing on my palm quite legibly. In mid-afternoon, while we sat together on the settee and my mother prayed for us upstairs, I proposed and held out my hand for the verdict. A firm and emphatic "Yes" was traced on my palm, and I had soon given Ruth the money to buy an engagement ring. We could not celebrate the occasion; I was unable to take her out to a show or a restaurant. She came up into the clay country on the three succeeding days and then travelled home to Weymouth with Bella, incredibly thrilled at having carried through one of the strangest missions which a woman had ever tried to accomplish. I was relieved that there was no opposition from her family. Bella and Mrs Peaty might be surprised and a little anxious about her prospects, but they noted the repetition of a pattern. Ruth's mother had married a war-shattered man, so she could hardly object to Ruth's choice of a handicapped husband. We were marrying on the same principle of an apparently blind faith in Providence, with the modest security of a Civil List pension—then £300 a year—and uncertain earnings from my books and occasional broadcasts.

The plans that filled our letters for the rest of the summer did not seem favourable to an ideal marriage. Ruth needed all the lessons she had learnt during those extraordinary eight years in which she had lived like a nun while still hoping to marry her devout marine. The spiritual sense of vocation had to replace romantic glitter and even some aspects of romantic gold. We could not have a honeymoon, and I could not offer her a separate home: we would have to live with my mother. Ruth was human enough to show traces of wistfulness and disappointment, remembering her early dreams as she roamed in Epping Forest before the war, the hazy flights of imagination calling her to a royal bower of love. She reminded me several times that the Brownings had enjoyed a wonderful honeymoon in Paris and Italy. But we knew our destiny, and I tried to make it as normal as possible. As the tenancy of the Goonamarris cottage could not be transferred to me until my mother's death, I attempted to rent a bigger house in the hamlet, and when Ruth came down in October to make final preparations for the wedding, the landlord took us over the premises, but he would only accept temporary rent on condition that I bought the house later, and the price was beyond my resources. We resigned ourselves to settling in my birthplace, and the owners agreed to modernise it and add a bathroom.

In the midst of this fret and hubbub I wrote "Wedding Eve" as my eve-of-marriage gift to Ruth. It summed up the essence of our situation, our special kind of revolt:

> "So two more loves are freed,
>   Outside an age adrift and dark:
>   Vigils of dune and forest
>   Set us on the anchoring quest,
>   And we find how disenchanted seed
>   Is changed to spirit's Cana-spark."

It was the old mystical-erotic theme which I had been presenting in various forms and moods ever since my teens: the contrast between natural love, which is so vulnerable, and love protected by divine grace through Christian faith. I had always seen the truth complete, but the inspiration had been partial and lopsided: I had been given either spiritual grace without

sex-appeal (as with Eileen) or romantic ardour without supernatural grace (as with Mary). Now there was a wholeness and
I could write with calm assurance, no longer striving towards
an unseen goal of unity. I had told one or two of my literary
friends that the wedding date was fixed, though we were trying
to keep it secret locally, as we did not want a crowd of uncom-
prehending villagers staring at us. Charles Causley had gladly
accepted my suggestion that he should be my best man, and
Derek Parker had offered to do a brief note on the marriage for
his diary column in *The Times*, thus giving it national publicity.

The wedding day—Saturday, 26 October—was mild, with
occasional rain and mist blurring the clay-peaks. A telegram of
congratulations from Monica Hutchings arrived early, taking
my thoughts lovingly back to Mappowder and Sherborne.
Bella and Mrs Peaty had lodged at Nanpean, and in mid-
morning I met Ruth's remarkable mother—a large, voluble,
energetic woman in her seventies, isolated by tragedy and
revealing a consequent disregard of the conventional pro-
prieties of dress and habit: one felt that she would have been
quite at home preaching in the Indian jungle, as she had meant
to amid the grief of her first widowhood. In contrast, an elegant,
hotel-haunting friend of Ruth's, Albert White, had motored
down from Middlesex to give her away. After lunch I was
aware that our little lounge was filling with guests. Familiar
hands shook mine as I sat at my desk, and I vaguely pictured
the person—the smooth-cheeked, bespectacled, immaculately
boyish Charles Causley, the lean shaggy Lionel Miskin (who
had left the Roman Catholic Church, become a pantheistic
humanist and published a novel). My foster-sisters Violet and
Frances kissed me, and I touched the silky hair of the children
Mandy and Margaret.

Just before the service was due to start we all went over to
Trethosa chapel in mixed groups, some riding in Miskin's van
None of the cars had white ribbons. My mother and I rode
with Charles Causley, and when we reached the lonely Bethel
on the hillside, stark among wet fields, I was surprised to learn
that a BBC television cameraman was awaiting us. Only a few

villagers were in the pews as Charles led me up the aisle. Ruth soon entered, looking young and radiant in a short peach-coloured crimplene dress, carrying a spray of cream roses and with a solitary rose nestling in her hair. We both felt very peaceful and relaxed, and the service was unusually simple, as I was allowed to recite the vows instead of repeating them, clause by clause, after the minister. I had memorised the responses and my mother stood behind me, tapping me at the appropriate moments. This was a great day for her, vindicating the faith she had held tenaciously for thirty years in defiance of the fate that made me unmarriageable. Perhaps as Charles Causley glanced out of the window at the grey mist softening Meledor clay-tips he recalled a letter I had sent him when I was in the throes of the T crisis, whimsically referring to "all this singeing of feathers mythical and mystical birds have to go through". In an account of the wedding which he broadcast two days later he quoted the poem T had inspired:

"Bless with your dreams my broken clay. . . ."

But Ruth was no teenager, and she was blessing me with something more substantial than dreams.

CHAPTER THIRTEEN

PHOENIX IN GRACE

AFTER THIRTEEN YEARS of blindness I still lived in a white fog that was tinged with brown or yellow when the sun shone. The bright colouring of my poetry may have been due partly to the fact that I had no experience of a world that was "dark amid the blaze of noon". The absence of darkness may also help to explain why I never said anything which blind people are supposed to say. A year or two before Mary cajoled me into learning Braille, the BBC invited me to speak in the special radio programme for the blind, "In Touch". Charles Causley came down and interviewed me, but when the London feature editor heard the tape she refused to broadcast it. I could only say that I had no interest in handicaps or in methods of over-coming them, that I had once been "a muddled sex-mystic", that "A Calvinist in Love" had poured out of me after I caught a smile from the schoolgirl milkmaid who brought a cabbage and a jug of milk to our door one Saturday in 1945, and that I was determined to be inspired only by happiness and therefore wrote nothing when I felt depressed. A few extracts from the interview were later broadcast in a West Region literary programme.

This refusal to think or write within handicaps is a vital clue to my work and my marriage. It made me feel normal enough to fit into the thought-patterns of a normal wife. I never left Ruth's world to study the training of blind and deaf people and become infected with the psychological pressures of the "sealed-off". Through will-power and imagination I escaped these pressures and grew increasingly flexible and objective in my poetry. The first poem I wrote after my marriage was about St Teresa, and the second, describing Ruth and myself at the valley bridge over the clay-stream in January 1969, contrasted my fulfilment with the emotional tragedies of Hardy and Keats. I never associated our peculiar habits with physical disabilities. Ruth would pause in a lane and scribble something on my palm about lorries or wagtails. She ate her breakfast, tea and supper sitting on a stool close to my chair at the desk, so that I could be aware of her presence. When visitors called, she sat on the stool for hours, transmitting any questions they might wish me to answer. I registered only the fact that I was now married and had a devoted companion who shared things with me. This positive reaction was, of course, more difficult for Ruth. The necessity of adapting herself to awkward and embarrassing practices, repeated every day, in public as well as private, was often a strain to her. There were other domestic problems, inevitable when a town-dweller tries to settle in a remote cottage with villagers who accept crude, countrified methods and tastes as the normal way of life. The early stages of our marriage were not free from tensions and crises, and we realised how essential was the spiritual motive which had led us to take the hazards of such a union. If we had married to express a modern sociological ideal, requiring an environment congenial to both parties, the stark predicament at Goona-marris would have shattered our dreams and our relationship before we had spent the first winter together.

We had agreed that Ruth should go back to Weymouth alone every spring and autumn for a short holiday with her mother and sister, and to relax amid familiar beauties as she roamed on the cliffs near her Rodwell home or sat reading or writing letters in the shade of the Tudor castle. I felt bewildered at the start of her first absence, wholly in my mother's care again, but it was a new thrill to receive letters addressed to "My own darling husband". The reunion was stimulating, and the poems spurted faster than at any previous period. I had seldom written more than six poems a year even before I went blind, but in 1969 I produced fourteen poems—about half of

The Echoing Tip. Some of them commemorated what Ruth called our "honeymoon" excursions to the Cornish coast during the summer.

The most significant of these was a visit to Alfred Wallis' grave at St Ives. We sat on the tombstone of this strange Salvationist fisherman and artist who had been haunted by visions of ships and harbours as he neared the end of his earthly voyage, the drab haven of Madron workhouse. He, too, had experienced an extraordinary marriage. As a youth of twenty he had married a middle-aged widow, and it was only after her death, when he was almost seventy, that he began frantically painting pictures on old cardboard box-lids. In his grief he had to preserve some symbol of "what use to be" (as he put it in his quaint English). . . . Ruth seemed very happy, pressing against me on the carved slab, looking down the sloping cemetery to Porthmeor beach and the grey Cornish sea that Wallis had so loved. She was not thinking simply of his paintings but of the Salvation Army band blaring triumphant defiance to his sad fate at the funeral here in 1942. I was thinking of "the 'Hallelujah' on the bridal stair" which brought him, in spite of his crude illiteracy, so close to our marital approach. I was moved by a deeper sense of affinity at Porthmeor than when I stood at the graves of Wordsworth and Ruskin, who had mounted the bridal stair with an uneasy conscience or a neurotic dread.

Later, when we went to Fowey, I merely enjoyed a boat trip up the river with Ruth, Mother and my vigorous, forthright cousin Annie. I did not visit Q's grave. I had once been half irritated and half amused by a newspaper report of a lecture given in London, in which I was included among the Cornish writers who worked "under the shadow of the great Q, who was an all-pervading influence". It was an absurd statement, for while Q may have influenced A. L. Rowse and Anne Treneer, his cool academic humanism and Victorian elegance could not impress the younger generation. I respected his fine service to Cornwall and Cambridge, but he could no more influence me than Pope could influence Blake. I had never found a true literary kinship in Cornwall, though I had found good friends to whose practical help I owed much. Rowse and John Rowland had praised my work, but Rowse was a rationalist, Rowland a Unitarian. My contemporaries, Charles Causley and Terence Tiller, and younger Cornish poets like D. M. Thomas, admired my creative vitality while disagreeing with my religious dogmas and the consequent inverted "rebel" attitude to life and art. They might pay tribute to Alfred Wallis' pictures, but they would not join me in asserting that the naïve faith which got him into heaven is more important than the naïve talent that got him into art galleries.

I had often been accused of despising Art, and I did despise the solemn stuff with a capital "A"; but, like Eric Gill, I had been forced into this resistance by the aesthete's arrogant claim to be above the discipline of Church creeds and morals. I valued art when it functioned in harmony with Christian truth, and when it expressed a humble, yearning spirit without belief, as in some of Hardy's and Day Lewis' poems. I also appreciated neutral art which merely conveys physical fact or experience without any pompous inflation of the artist's rôle, as in the descriptive poems of D. H. Lawrence and much of Dylan Thomas' work. But my Evangelical-Catholic mysticism made me a lone wolf in Cornish art circles. From the time of my marriage I had worshipped regularly at Trethosa chapel, and this involved some pleasant ironies—the thrill of composing poems about the Virgin and saints as I sat in my old Wesleyan pew, and never feeling that there was the least incongruity between my poem and the sermon that Ruth was trying to communicate to me.

There might seem to be a more baffling inconsistency in my acceptance of a Cornish Gorsedd bardship in 1970. Helena Charles had sorrowed over my strictures on Cornish nationalism in *Confession of a Rebel*, and as the years passed my hostility had softened to indifference. If some people in the duchy wished to learn Cornish and get excited about ancient earthworks and cromlechs and the Arthurian legends I had no objection, but I had other things to absorb my interest. I had refused two previous offers of a bardship for my poetry, in 1961 and 1966, and would probably have refused the third if I had not married. But I felt that I could not deny Ruth a memorable afternoon out, an event that would bring a little colour and romantic pageantry to break the monotonous routine of housework, palm-writing and dreary walks among industrial litter at Goonamarris.

The 1970 Gorsedd was held at St Piran's Round, near Perranporth beach, and on that grey September afternoon my cousin Annie drove me with Ruth and Mother along muddy lanes almost to the Atlantic shore. We went first to a small Methodist chapel where the bards put on their flowing blue robes. I remained bare-headed until the initiation, carrying my hood on my arm. A Gorsedd official took Ruth and me in his car to the grassy amphitheatre where the ceremony was performed, while my mother and Annie joined the crowd of sightseers. I did not march in the bardic procession or stand in the bardic circle. Ruth and I sat on chairs opposite the raised dais where the Grand Bard, trumpeter, harpist and Queen of Cornwall were gathered. We waited quietly, thankful that rain was holding off. The weird blasts of the horn of peace were sounded and a lot of Cornish was chanted or sung, then my name was called and Ruth led me across the bumpy turf to the dais. The Grand Bard bent forward and welcomed me in Cornish as he enclosed my clasped hands between his. A minute or two later Ruth made Gorsedd history as the only woman who has ever "crowned" her husband with the bardic hood. Over a thousand spectators in the grandstand and at other vantage points watched her tug the large blue cowl-like hood into position and adjust the black band across my forehead. Mother looked proudly towards us, sitting on a stool beside Annie, but she had now developed cataract and could not see us at that distance. Ruth's action was, of course, allowed only because of my blindness, but I thought it beautifully symbolic, showing that we represented the mystical love I wrote about, and that I was not merely acknowledging myself to be a Cornishman.

We came home with a glow of achievement and expansion, and this was heightened a few days later when I posted the completed manuscript of *The Echoing Tip* to my publishers. Before Christmas the book was accepted and Ruth could feel that her sacrifice of family ties and all the amenities of Weymouth had not been a pitiful waste. The large number of dramatic monologues in the collection revealed that I was getting nearer to the Browning pattern both as a man and as a poet. My Civil List pension had been doubled and we had no financial worries. The whole situation proved the fallacy of the popular idea that poverty, loneliness and frustration are good stimulants for an artist. I had always found them cramping, suffocating and distorting. While a poet is fighting desperately to make his vision work, he will mis-state or overstate his case and present a faith bleared by the smoke of battle. This may give his writings a strange originality, but it makes him less reliable as a guide and teacher. It is only after he has demonstrated that his vision works, when he is living it on the everyday bread-and-butter level, that he can say exactly what he means without a false note or a warped emphasis.

The publication of *The Echoing Tip* in the autumn of 1971 was accompanied in the West Country by a BBC television film—the first in which I had appeared as a husband. The Gorsedd initiation had been given a minute's space in a regional newsreel: I was shown with Ruth as the Grand Bard conferred on me the Cornish name, Prydyth an Pry (Poet of Clay). Now in the film about my new book I was seen as a clay phoenix with no trace of emotional singeing. Ruth told viewers how she had been guided to marry me through prayer, and my mother supported this with a moving religious testimony. Both their statements were re-broadcast in the national "Pick of the Week" radio programme. Our unusual love story became widely known during that winter, though in a society that was largely pagan or materialistic the average viewer and the average poetry-lover must have found it hard to understand our kind of marriage—startlingly unconventional ("We have laughed at prudence," I wrote in my Fowey poem), yet owing its stability to Evangelical faith. We saw our fulfilment chiefly as evidence for the God Whom Browning had proclaimed in *The Ring and the Book*—the objective Interventionist

"Who, for our own good, makes the need extreme,
    Till at the last He puts forth might and saves."

The closing poem in the collection, a tribute to Karl Barth, was a retort to the radical clergy who seemed so frightened of the whole idea of divine intervention. I affirmed Christianity as I had known it—a descending flame that liberated the phoenix:

"A love fire-tongued, cleaving our sin,
    Retrieving the soul from racial evolution,
    Giving it grace to mortify,
    In deeps or shallows, all projections of the divine."

My attitude to organised religion was more complex than the benevolent tolerance I felt towards the Cornish Celtic revival. I still detested those sections of the Church which denied or diluted the supernatural. The success of my "impossible" marriage made me realise the silliness of projecting an image of a God who had conveniently died so that man could come of age. Such "coming of age" had brought a flood of divorces, so it was obviously wiser to remain childlike and dependent and let the Almighty do the projecting. All relief from strain in our home came in answer to prayer. Ruth had missed in Cornwall the vital and varied religious fellowship she had enjoyed in Weymouth, and after two years at Goonamarris the spiritual isolation grew intolerable to her. She prayed explicitly for "a Christian friend with a car". Soon afterwards, in the autumn of 1970, she found a true affinity in Gwen Pearce, a Newquay bookseller who conducted a service at Trethosa chapel one Sunday evening and, in conversing with Ruth at the close of it, became aware of her loneliness and need. Gwen was a tall, sensitive woman in her fifties, the wife of a businessman who carried text-banners around the streets and beaches. She began motoring up to Goonamarris every Wednesday, taking Ruth out for drives, introducing her to Evangelical groups at Newquay, Bodmin, Truro and St Austell. We also received visits from Miss Oates, an aged mystical lady who led a spiritual healing group at Truro. I had started corresponding with Sister Mary Agnes, the Roman Catholic nun-poet, whose serene letters were in marked contrast to the emotional tension revealed in her poems. My faith was fed from many sources, and I was thankful when in 1972 I was asked to revise *The Invading Gospel* for a paperback edition. This enabled me to make the book more complete and balanced.

Our life seemed to settle into a quiet and pleasant rhythm in the fourth year of our marriage. I continued to produce poems for my next collection, *Broad Autumn*, and wrote an occasional essay. We often strolled down to a new artificial waterfall we had discovered in the edge of Tregargus Wood. The stream had been diverted because of clay-work expansion in the valley, and milk-white liquid now poured over a high mass of granite boulders, plunging and swirling into the gorge. It was a novel and picturesque sight with the wild shaggy slopes curving away southward, bearing the holly trees which I was no longer able to cut. But Ruth pined for the sea, and during the summer we went several times to Frances' bungalow at St Columb Minor and tramped out across the fields to Porth, which became our favourite Cornish beach, the only one described in detail in my poetry. I always got my trousers soaking wet through deep paddling with Ruth in the massive breakers. We would lie or sit on the sands until I had dried a little, while my cousin Annie fetched ice-cream for us. In the autumn came the usual ten days' absence, Ruth in Weymouth, with the compensation of writing and receiving more love letters. On Christmas Day we were all back at Frances' home, and the atmosphere was calm and cheerful as the year closed.

But early in 1973 a dark threat suddenly chilled us. Ruth learnt from her sister that Mrs Peaty had been taken seriously ill with complications of dropsy and a strange psychological snap which destroyed her will to live and made her refuse food. Ruth hurried to Weymouth in bleak mid-winter weather, and we were all gripped by suspense and anxiety. She could only send me brief notes about her mother's condition, hospital visits, and Bella's anxiety about the situation. After nearly a fortnight she returned to Cornwall exhausted, torn between the two loyalties. At Goonamarris were her blind husband and half-blind mother-in-law, who was now in her eightieth year. In Weymouth was her stricken mother, with Bella struggling to cope and prepare for any emergency while maintaining her office job. The sense of crisis was a heavy strain and inhibited my writing. In March Ruth was summoned to Rodwell again because the situation had deteriorated. I spent a sad fifty-seventh birthday, alone with my mother. Ruth's notes told of desperate efforts to find new hospital accommodation, and she stayed in Dorset until this had been provided. She came back to the clay country looking pale and worn, and each day was tinged with dread as she awaited Bella's reports. Then on the morning of 16 April, Gwen Pearce arrived and broke as gently as possible the news she had just received over the telephone from Bella. Mrs Peaty had died a few hours earlier. Ruth was conscience-smitten and full of grief as she left me once more, this time to attend the funeral. I wrote the tribute "A Mother's Tragedy" during her absence, and did all I could to console and strengthen her, but several months passed before she regained her usual high spirits and the innocent elfish "sauciness" (as she called it) which had made me nickname her "Pixie".

In November came a further strain when my mother went into Truro hospital for a cataract operation. She seemed bright and confident on the evening we visited her, and apparently enjoyed her stay in the ward, chatting and laughing with the other patients. The operation was successful, but for the rest of her life she had great difficulty in focusing and had to wear thick, cumbrous glasses with one lens frosted. As soon as the operation scar had healed, however, she began a task which she felt to be God's final commission to her. It was now her habit to remain in bed until mid-morning, and I never suspected that she was struggling to set down on paper a record of her encounter with God and its effect on my life and work. Ruth knew that she was attempting the task, that she was often dissatisfied and depressed, tearing up page after page, feeling that the weaknesses of old age made her unfit to write such a testimony. I was kept in ignorance until, in the autumn of 1974, Mother told me that Gwen Pearce was typing the manuscript. She explained that she had wanted the undertaking to be a personal matter between God and herself: she had probably feared that I would be telling her what to say and how to say it. The little memoir, entitled *I Proved Thee at the Waters*, was published in 1976 by a religious firm in Derbyshire. It was a remarkable feat for an uneducated village woman of eighty, and though it contained a few slips of memory its message was clear and challenging.

While Mother was engaged on this document we were all cheered by the acceptance of *Broad Autumn*. This book, published in the seventh year of our marriage, was a wedding anniversary volume, dedicated to Ruth. It consisted largely of poems about marriage and the natural alternatives of rape and prostitution, and closed with a dramatic monologue spoken by Ruth, suggesting our varied experiences:

> "Sun-strut, prick of mists,
>   Thunder on tin tabernacles,
>   Moon-glide on cavern votaries."

The inclusion of "tin tabernacles" revealed our sympathy with Alfred Wallis' religion, while the "cavern votaries" in Bernadette's grotto had become part of our spiritual world through Ruth's marking the sign of the Cross on my forehead with Lourdes water. My allusive imagist style gave fresh evidence that T. S. Eliot and Dylan Thomas were more congenial to me than the neatly traditional poets. I did not find these two modern rebels unintelligible when they had something to say. I responded vividly to the portions of their work that were written in English: the poetry became meaningless only when they tried to be purely technical and clever, with no emotional drive. To me, Dylan Thomas communicated the pangs of sex and death more poignantly (because less sentimentally) than Keats. He presented a rural or sea-powered counterpart of Eliot's urban "waste land" where the cheap typist "puts a record on the gramophone" to ease boredom after casual copulation. But in *Ash Wednesday* there was a spiritual poignancy beyond Thomas' range. I had long regarded this sequence as the greatest penitential poem written in my lifetime. It confirmed the impression I had gained from Donne—that the poetry of Christian experience never reflects the fashion of any age, but is always offensive to contemporary fashions. Browning and Hopkins reached back to Donne and forward to Eliot in the timeless movement of personal regeneration, the emergence from egotism into a sense of unworthiness, the humble and contrite heart that can only cast itself on divine mercy:

> "Suffer me not to be separated
> And let my cry come unto Thee."

I did not find this a negative or ascetic prayer. It was the attitude in which I had received Ruth—indeed, a prayer of this sort had always been my response to amorous pleasure, and this had made my poetry more complex than that of the romantics and the cynical realists. They extolled or satirised an over-simplified emotion, an instinct separated from theological truth, so that the winds of the spirit were stifled by the "pneumatic bliss" (as Eliot called it) of the body. A reviewer had said that my main theme was "sanctification through sexual love", but there was always the presupposition of Christian faith which carried the theme beyond my own personality. I was not showing what a handicapped man might be forced to feel or believe as a "compensation phantasy". I was speaking for the central tradition of Christendom, especially the robust

British pattern. This fact had been brought home to me very poignantly when, with Ruth sitting beside me on a stool, I had listened to the broadcast of Princess Anne's wedding in Westminster Abbey, and then written a poem to express "what the English meant by marriage". Even though most of my contemporaries meant something very different, the sacramental challenge persisted.

CHAPTER FOURTEEN

OVER THE BORDER

THE GRANITE COTTAGE at Goonamarris, with the modern bathroom unit stuck on incongruously at one corner, was no longer on a frontier. The view from the front windows had become as scarred and clotted as that at the back. Ruth looked out from our bedroom on to a car park and a wall of rubble edged with spiral tracks, up which the heavy transport lorries lurched every day to make the mess higher and broader. The new method of taking waste material to the dumping sites in lorries, instead of spilling it from rope-hauled tip-waggons at the apex of a cone, had nothing of the fantasy, the poetic and even erotic appeal of the old clay-pyramids. As I was blind and married, the change made no difference to me apart from restricting our walks, but Ruth found the hideous oblong mounds and spluttering vehicles depressing and soul-deadening. She still required the emotional stimulus of beauty, and this fitted in with the complex nature of our long search for each other.

The element of search in my life had been almost entirely erotic. I never had to seek God any more than Francis Thompson had to seek the Hound of Heaven, and I was not the sort of mystic whose quest is narrowly and negatively religious. From the time I first heard of the Manichean and Gnostic heresies I loathed them, for I had proved that sense impressions are vital media of spiritual experience. I had noticed, for example, that mystical awareness was especially keen at twilight when the landscape showed unearthly and marginal transitions. The withdrawal of colour and the shifting density of shadow created

an atmosphere in which a higher dimension of life breathed
and palpitated. This was not nature mysticism, since the
landscape was industrial, but I usually had some girl in mind
and the blurred white clay-breasts affected me as they might
have affected D. H. Lawrence, except that for me the female
image was sharp and healthy, not suggesting lotus and swoon
but prompting a prayer for Christian marriage.

Ruth's early response to the mysterious play of light and
shade in Epping Forest had something in common with this,
the same background and context of faith, vaguely romantic,
though in telling me of her past she laid more stress on her
mature apprehensions in Old Castle Gardens in Weymouth.
The spiritual potency of the scene became very strong after
the wreck of her dream about the marine. She would steal
away to the cliff where evening dusk included the changed
face and cadence of the sea and Portland looked detached and
cloistered across the harbour, guarding her nun-like absorption
in other-worldly love. It was a phase of purgation more extreme
than any I had known. I could never understand the motives or
feelings of monks until I married and lost my fear of celibacy.
But even for Ruth the split vision fused again, and in the same
setting of palms and roses she nourished the "nymph-ardour
and dogma-flash" as twin signals for her future husband. The
fulfilment among Cornish clay-pits was an irony that seemed
to link up, not with Rodwell and Epping Forest, but with the
stark London home of her childhood.

Since her mother died Ruth's thoughts had strayed back
more frequently to those crisis-ridden years. As she sat beside
me on her stool after breakfast or supper, she would scribble
on my palm an account of some tragic episode that was fretting
her memory. At the age of five she was playing in the garden
one day when an ambulance stopped outside the gate and
strange people entered the house. A lady ordered her to come
indoors, giving her no time even to pick up her doll. Frightened
and bewildered, she was told that she and her sister were being
taken to a children's home at Wanstead. Mrs Peaty had
suffered a physical and psychological collapse following the

birth and death of her fourth child, and had to go into hospital for treatment. The war-broken William would try to manage for himself until his wife recovered, but he could not take care of the two girls. Ruth's anguish and panic in the official refuge-centre were counterparts of the terrors I had endured during my first spell of semi-blindness when I was five. Her mother remained in hospital for several months, then came back to shoulder the domestic burden afresh. Her unrelieved battle for her children, especially for her son Jack when he was slipping into schizophrenia and after he was placed in the care of doctors, was an epic of faith and maternal love similar to my mother's battle for me. But the results were less apparent, and her brave spirit was sometimes troubled by religious question-ings. She had accompanied Bella to Cornwall each summer for four years after Ruth's marriage, though I only had brief contacts with her on these occasions, as she lodged at Violet's home at St Dennis and went off on bus trips with Ruth from there. Her swollen legs prevented her from walking far, and at the coast, Porthpean or Mevagissey, she would sit brooding and wistful on a bench while Ruth and Bella climbed the cliffs or explored the quays. . . . And then the pattern had snapped and Bella had to travel alone to see us and Ruth found the Wey-mouth house strangely silent and empty when she returned to it.

There was some compensation at Goonamarris, for our isolated existence was enlivened by many visitors. A few of Ruth's relatives and old friends called on us while on holiday in Cornwall, including her Weymouth foster-parents, Mr and Mrs Wilkins, a kindly and devoted Brethren couple, and their daughters. My work attracted an increasing number of teachers and students to our cottage. A Scots girl student had unwittingly prompted me to cast my religious poem "Broad Autumn" in the imagery of braes, lochs and glens—a curious irony, as the girl was an atheist. Various authors and journalists found their way to our remote hamlet. Derek Savage still motored or cycled up from Mevagissey to discuss comparative religion with Ruth and Mother. In the autumn of 1974 John Rowland, the Unitarian, paid us his first visit, bringing his warm-hearted Anglican wife. I had corresponded with Rowland intermittently for thirty-eight years, though we were poles apart in temperament and faith. He had been trained as a scientist and rationalist, had written thrillers and a book of liberal religious analysis, *One Man's Mind*. He was affable, a good mixer, and in his Unitarian ministry almost quixotically tolerant of every sort of belief—Calvinist, Hindu or Buddhist—that people could use as a psychological prop. All our visitors admired Ruth's intelligence, her vivacity and her cooking, and found me friendly and human despite my inability to converse with them.

My mother was usually cheerful in company, but she had grown very frail and shrunken, weakened by blood pressure and hardening of arteries. She had occasional bouts of depression. My late marriage had brought her psychological and emotional problems which she was too old to cope with. For fifty years she had looked after me in her own way, buying the sort of clothes she wanted me to wear, setting before me the sort of food she wanted me to eat at the hours that suited her. She realised that a younger woman, London-born and unconventional, would have tastes very different from hers, but in practice she did not find it easy to accept the changes in my dress, diet and general habits. All through the decades of frustration when one girl after another threw me back on her hands, she had been determined not to fail me, determined to live and keep active for my sake. But now that I was happily married she seemed to feel that her life had lost its point: her driving force had gone, and she was inwardly confused. Her true self was deeply thankful for my marriage, and she made this clear when she wrote in her booklet: "It is such a joy to have a daughter-in-law who so completely understands my son and so faithfully devotes her life to him." But at times her tenacious maternal instinct made her long to be back in the old days when I was exclusively in her care, giving her existence a purpose and meaning.

She was also burdened with the inevitable loneliness of the aged, the sense of being "left behind". All her brothers and sisters, and most of her school friends, were dead. Her last surviving sister, Annie Greenslade, had died in 1971, and now her niece, Annie Julian—my freckled, forthright cousin who had taken us on so many trips in her car—had developed cancer and would never drive a car again. This restricted Mother's movements, as she could not walk to a bus-stop, and we had to make new arrangements about summer outings. In August 1975 Violet's husband, Morley, took us to Frances' bungalow and Ruth and I enjoyed our usual paddle at Porth. A little later Morley took us to Bedruthan, where the ancient cliff-steps, the only means of access to the beach, had recently been re-opened to the public. Mother stayed on the grassy slope with Violet while I cautiously descended the long, twisting flight of steps with Ruth, Frances and Raymond Brown. After paddling we were almost trapped by the tide, which came swirling around the base of the exit while other parts of the beach were still dry. Having dashed back to the steps just in time, I had to climb the cliff-face and at one bend nearly put my foot over the edge. Ruth grabbed me frantically and held on until we reached the summit. Mother was very relieved when we joined her: she was always afraid that in strange places with Ruth—as with Mary in Lakeland—I would be "too venturesome".

But though there were shadows and difficulties in Mother's closing years, the triumph of her faith was widely recognised, and in many ways 1976 was the crowning year of her life. In April *I Proved Thee at the Waters* was published, and a month later she was honoured at the Trethosa chapel centenary celebrations. Being the oldest member of the chapel she proudly cut the centenary cake, and forty copies of her booklet, donated by herself, were sold in the vestry. In November she was interviewed by the BBC about her pamphlet, and five short broadcasts were made from her remarks. This testimony was her last public utterance. Early in 1977 she received head injuries through a fall indoors, and though she seemed to recover she was obviously shaken and worn out. She carried on bravely for three months, and during the final week of May she tried to manage the house and do the cooking while Ruth was ill with influenza.

On the evening of Friday, 3 June, Mother led me out for a brief walk to the Slip, moving very slowly and stiffly in the warm sunshine. I kissed her good-night and had no premonitions. Next morning I went into her bedroom to greet her as usual, but this time her hand did not reach out to welcome me. I touched her, but she remained motionless. I then called Ruth, who immediately telephoned for a doctor, asking me to massage Mother's shrivelled little body. We supposed that she was unconscious after a stroke, but when the doctor arrived he said she had been dead for an hour. While we were still dazed with shock the postman delivered an acceptance of my poem "Unearthed", which contained an apt message for this desolating moment, stressing the power of faith to repudiate

> "negative awe, the false reverence
> For tragic ends, the sense of an ultimate
> In the earth's clutch at our worn-out clothing."

The grief and regret were bitter, but even before we left the bedside I was aware that the suddenness of the bereavement was merciful. How could I, blind and deaf, have coped with death-bed scenes? Ruth had not been well lately, and might have collapsed under the strain of nursing Mother through months of invalidism and recurring crises.

Neither of us believed in gloomy conventions about death. We did not draw the curtains or wear less colourful clothes. I wore my brown-striped wedding suit at the funeral on the following Thursday. The service at Trethosa chapel seemed remote, only half-realised as I sat with Ruth while Derek Savage paid tribute to "our dear sister-in-Christ" and my other literary friends—Charles Causley, Ernest Martin and Lionel Miskin—sympathised, quiet and subdued in their pews. Heavy rain poured on the chapel, and on St Stephen's churchyard when presently we walked behind the coffin. I liked the feel of my wet hair and overcoat: I had always loved rain and did not find it mournful. I was, in fact, vaguely reminded of the rain that had pelted me as I strolled with Mother and Mary on the bank of Lake Windermere. Only Ruth's tight, consoling clutch on my arm made this walk, as far as my senses were concerned, any different from the ramble on soaked paths and turf at Adelaide's Hill in 1964. The radical difference lay in my numbed emotions, in the strong pervading aura of gratitude that I was married.

Among those who attended the funeral were two new friends who did much to help us during the painful period of adjustment. They were Pat Moyer, an American professor employed by Exeter University, and her husband, James Morgan. They had recently visited us to arrange a one-day seminar on my art and ideas at St Austell. Pat was a rare, exuberant woman, warmly spontaneous in her affection and critical insight. She had made a special study of Blake and was, as she put it, "unclubbable". James blended Celtic gentleness—he was Cornish—with sound practical sense. Their home was a converted chapel near a beach on the south Cornish coast, and during the month after Mother's funeral, while Bella was staying with us, they came up to Goonamarris several times and took us out for drives. I paddled at Watergate Bay with their pretty and precocious little daughter, Cerris, then four years old. James fetched me, with Ruth and Bella, to the seminar at a St Austell college, where I signed copies of Mother's booklet, feeling the poignancy, as she had intended to be there to sign them herself. I answered students' questions, my brief replies being amplified by Ruth and a young teacher friend of ours, Andrew Symons, who had remarkable affinities with me in temperament and mystical stress.

When Bella returned to Weymouth in July, Ruth found our cottage even more silent and oppressive than her Rodwell house had seemed in the autumn of 1973. I wrote no poems for four months after my mother died, though I had virtually finished another collection just before the blow fell. A public reading of my poetry in the Chapter House of Truro Cathedral was being organised by Margaret Shirley, a cultured Anglican who brought the mystical Miss Oates to our cottage and was very keen on promoting my work. A visit we paid to her home in 1976 had inspired my poem, "In a Truro Garden". There were many hitches in arranging the programme, but the recital, which included piano and violin renderings of classical music, took place in September. I enjoyed once more the pleasant flavour of irony, sitting with Ruth under the episcopal spires while Douglas Leach's trained voice read poems I had written when I was a raw individualist and distrusted churches. But he also read a new poem, "The Restored See", which I had composed, at the invitation of the Bishop of St Germans, to mark the diocesan centenary. The bishop and the dean welcomed me, and I was conscious that a tide of reconciliation had flooded over the warped and crusty angles of my youthful prejudice. I knew that some of my more politically-minded friends were a trifle worried about my open link with the ecclesiastical system. One of them—the Essex journalist Bernard Smith, who had visited me in 1951 after being stirred by *Confession of a Rebel*—had launched a campaign against the infiltration of Communism into the Establishment and the World Council of Churches. I was concerned only with resisting materialism, and cared little whether it was Left or Right in its political jargon. It was obvious that the clergy who supported my work were not radicals, for no radical would want the kind of faith or the kind of marriage I advocated.

I came home from the cathedral feeling that I was not entirely without honour in my own county, and a week later I was in Weymouth on an incredible visit. A couple of Ruth's friends—Maurice Gabb, a fervent, visionary young man, and his practical Christian wife, Jean—had fetched us in their car, and I was back in my enchanted Dorset, seeing the complete pattern, understanding the strange prophetic thrill which had haunted me there in 1950. This time I entered Hardy's land from the west instead of the north, reaching Dorchester after nightfall and turning south along the lanes that twisted towards the coast. Incessant rain was beating in across Weymouth harbour as the car, bearing my typewriter and tape-recorder, skirted the bleared quays and climbed the sloping streets and avenues to the suburb of Rodwell. We alighted where South-lands Road slanted downhill again and a steep, stony track branched off, leading to Old Castle Gardens. The summer heat had gone, but our broad autumn held no threat of decay. We were to spend three weeks in Hardy's Budmouth, discover-ing fresh buds and no withered leaves in our relationship. Here in Ruth's home I could feel her roots as soon as I stepped into the cosy lounge, and in a day or two the whole house was as familiar to me as my Goonamarris cottage. Ruth had bought a new desk for me, and when I arrived it stood empty near the window that looked out on to the back garden. At this desk I was soon typing letters and cards to various friends who had attended the Truro recital, including Derek and Connie Savage and a half-blind and deaf young social worker, Pat Robins, who had sat with me for a few minutes while Ruth went into another room with Councillor Robins, Pat's husband, to test a recording he had made for us.

I was also to write at that desk the first poem I produced outside Cornwall—"Chesil Beach", a descriptive and philo-sophical poem which bore no trace of the pangs of bereavement. I missed Mother, but grief could not inspire me and I was being carried beyond it. The verse-rhythms came spontaneously, some of them thrusting up through a quiet service at the Baptist church to which Maurice took us. In an article pub-lished in *Unicorn* in 1961 I had written: "The mental tension and congestion which a poet suffers when half-a-dozen versions of the same line are all struggling to be born at once, knotting and twisting and bumping each other, is enough to drive one schizophrenic." But this was true only during the period when the phoenix was being badly singed, when my emotions were negative. It showed the pernicious effect of prolonged strain and unhappiness on a sensitive mind. A brain stung and bruised by misfortune can only work slowly and painfully, often in confusion, but this is not its normal creative state. Most of the poems Mary inspired had come fairly easily, and since my marriage I had certainly never composed a poem that threatened to split me. Erotic fulfilment had removed the psychological snags. From the new vantage-point, Ruth's base, where she had first read my books and letters, I could appreciate the marvel of it all—"my life of wonders", as Browning testified.

Bella kept a patient and humorous eye on me during Ruth's absences, and I was surprised that everything seemed so natural without my having to adapt myself to it by any conscious effort. The weather cleared, and Ruth and I sat under the glossy palm trees in her beloved Castle Gardens, exchanging remarks about Anne Boleyn and her faithless Bluebeard (of whom the Tudor castle crumbling on the cliff-edge reminded us), and about Ruth's more justifiable confidence as she walked along the ancient flagstones, past the goldfish-ruffled pond and the stripped sundial, on the eve of her leaving Weymouth to marry me. We would climb up or down the short flights of steps, moving from one bench to another so that Ruth could view the sea from various angles and tell me what she was looking at—a helicopter hovering and buzzing above Portland naval base, a steamer ploughing out into Weymouth harbour, bound for the Channel Islands. It all made me realise that I was a hundred miles from Cornwall, but I felt no pang of exile or homesickness. I hadn't seen Cornwall for twenty years, and even before my sight failed I had reacted against its harsh industrialism—first through Eileen's influence, then through my visit to the Powyses. In recent phases of my writing I had found the symbols of the Cornish coast more apt than those of the clay-pits, and now as Ruth took me down to the little cove under Sandsfoot Castle and we paddled there, I noticed the difference between the gentle Dorset ripples and the heavy Atlantic surf that pounded in at Porth and Bedruthan. I did not feel that I had lost my true environment. I suppose I was too much of a mystic to have exclusive regional ties. I responded to the divine mystery of form and purpose, mediated through the beloved woman in her own world, and it was even more powerful here than it had been in the Lake District, for Ruth had proved her devotion during nine years of marriage.

Sometimes Bella came with us to take snapshots, and one afternoon we scrambled down a cliff-rut from the gardens and trudged a mile or two across paths and roads to the Wyke Regis bungalow where Ruth's war-time foster-mother, Mrs Wilkins, now a widow in her eighties, lived alone. I also renewed my acquaintance with the two friends of Ruth's who had brought her to Cornwall for the wedding—Mary King, a genial maternity ward auxiliary, with whom Ruth had spent a holiday in the Welsh mountains, and Gwen Barnard, a former nanny, gentle and sympathetic. Mary gave us a breezy ride in her car when we visited Ruth's brother Jack in a rural inland hospital. He was a tall, slim, sensitive-looking man in his late forties, obviously pleased to see us, but tragically submerged and withdrawn. He led me across the tree-shadowed, freshly-mown grass and the wide gritty spaces of the hospital grounds and was able to write lucid greetings and thanks on my hand. The hospital was several miles east of Dorchester, and on the way back to Weymouth we halted at the Hardy memorial statue and I was photographed touching the carved hat. I thought the hat a wry symbol of Hardy's early faith, dropped uselessly on his knee instead of protecting his head from foul weather.

Perhaps the most striking and significant incident of all was the one I described in my poem—the evening when, having slithered amid the huge freak pebbles of Chesil Beach, we climbed to the summit of Portland and tramped over the flat ridge to attend a service in the Verne prison. Bella was a member of a choir that occasionally sang in the prison chapel, and as relatives of hers we were given permission to enter the penal settlement. A crisp flamboyant sunset flushed the western sky and the broad seascape, then softly faded into dusk as we drew near the grim walls. Our names were checked at the gate, and I was soon ushered into a unique, moving, unforgettable experience, sitting on a hard wooden chair among scores of convicts, the chaplain, warders and governor close to me, the atmosphere relaxed and cheerful. The prisoners clapped vigorously after a girl soloist challenged them with guitar-powered swing songs about God. They listened quietly to a brief pungent talk by the preacher who led the team. Ruth scribbled on my palm as she had done in Truro Cathedral, and I felt the aptness, the polarisation of the contrast. I belonged to both worlds—the refinements of religion and culture, and the raw humanity for which redemption must be a crude flame. I knew what a depth of understanding and kinship I would feel if I could look into the faces of these men, all of whom had battled with the dark sensual fires. When the guests were conducted out into the calm October night, I realised that I had reached a new level of liberty and resurgence. Ruth and I stood hand-in-hand outside the prison gate, breathing the pure air that eddied in from the sea on three sides, while the unseen waves rubbed along the flanks of Portland to their strange encounter with Chesil Beach.

CHAPTER FIFTEEN

PALMS AND THE PALACE

AFTER THIS FIRST visit to Weymouth Ruth and I returned home, very reluctantly, to an empty cottage and an atmosphere which, had we been conventional, would have suggested deep mourning. The new grave in St Stephen's churchyard was still rather unreal to me, as I had never seen it or heard the clods thud in it, but I knew it was there and that its effect on my attitude to Cornwall would be momentous. Handicaps and theology had lifted me from the simple heartbreak of a personal loss. My mother had lost much of her material individuality for me when I went blind, and even more when I married. I could not be solemn, much less morbid, about death where the bond between me and the deceased person was chiefly spiritual. Soon after our stay in Dorset Ruth took me to the Cornish cemetery and I wrote whimsically in my diary: "Ate ice-cream at Mum's grave. Did she smile?" My faith had moved steadily towards an outlook that often seemed frivolous, though it had a firm logical foundation—the idea, implied in some of Browning's poems and expounded in Chesterton's *Orthodoxy*, that man's tragedy is shallow compared with God's comedy. I believed Christians could share His comedy and be freed from the sense of being victims.

I did not so much feel that my mother had become dead to me as that the Cornwall she represented had gone dead. From my infancy onward she had provided the aura of security from which I looked out on the gloomy clayscape, the chapel, the sea to which she took me in summer. Now that she had vanished all this was stripped of a private, reassuring idiom. I could not transfer it and make it wholly Ruth's world; I could only affirm with every instinct of my heart and imagination, that the Weymouth area was now my world. I wished to record the last phase of my Cornish life and then slip quietly across the Tamar.

I began writing this book at the end of 1977, scribbling small portions in notebooks and then typing them myself (I preferred typing to dictation), nearly every day until the following spring. I took the manuscript with me on our second visit to Ruth's old home in May, and posted it to a publisher just before we caught a train to Bournemouth. I felt damped and uncertain in that town, missing the Weymouth features which were becoming so familiar and unique to me.

The outstanding event of this second holiday, however, was a pilgrimage to Hardy's birthplace. Maurice Gabb took us with his wife and children, and I felt a strange fascination and fitness as we tramped through Bockhampton woods. I tried to visualise the scene from the descriptions of it I had read in *Under the Greenwood Tree*. The bare cottage seemed surprisingly friendly, not at all sinister and depressing in its clean mellow surfaces. The homestead and the surrounding copse appeared to reflect the humility of Hardy's search for faith. It was this absence of pride and superiority in Hardy's scepticism that kept me sympathetic to most of his work. He recognised his own blindness.

On the homeward journey that day we stopped at a turfed slope where a stream pattered by, and during the picnic I was amused to learn that Maurice's younger daughter, seven-year-old Naomi, was walking around with her eyes shut, pretending to be blind "like Uncle Jack." She was too shy to romp with me as yet, but in later years she became the closest of my young Weymouth friends. She, with her sister Sharon and her two brothers, prompted me to write some comic children's verse, published in *The Bouncing Hills* in 1983, and as a teenager she inspired one or two of my serious religious poems.

Although Hardy was now my chief literary magnet in Dorset, I had not forgotten my old affinity with T. F. Powys, and before leaving the county Ruth and I went to Mappowder to pay our respects at his grave. The remote village churchyard was overgrown, and Ruth and her friend searched in vain for the relevant tombstone. At last Ruth questioned a tall middle-aged man who happened to be passing, and found to her astonishment that he was Powys's nephew, Gerard Casey, himself a writer of speculative plays and essays. He showed us the grave, and then on learning my identity he took us to his home and introduced us to his wife Mary, a lonely poet of the Emily Dickinson type, and also Powys's aged sister Lucy, who lived next door. Our friendship with this remarkable family was renewed each summer until the women died. Later Gerard gave us extensive car rides around rural Dorset, especially the Chaldon heaths were Powys had lived as a meditative hermit.

Back in Cornwall, the pace became more modern and bustling as the year advanced. The BBC had decided to make a television film of my early life, and preliminary investigators were sent to the clay area. Ruth and I and some of my old schoolmates were interviewed. The producer, Norman Stone, arrived in April 1979 and began hunting for the local cast. Robert Duncan, a St Austell actor who had known spiritual struggle and was groping towards faith, was selected to impersonate me, and Cerris Morgan-Moyer was chosen to play the part of the child Barbara.

Cerris had been drawn closer to us through a freak adventure at Christmas. Pat Moyer and her husband had brought her up from Portholland to see us, but they were caught in a sudden heavy snowstorm which marooned them at our cottage for two days. Cerris slept on our lounge settee, while her parents spent uncomfortable nights on the draughty floor. We all found some compensation for the mishap. Ruth and Pat discussed high cultural matters against the background of a swirling blizzard.

The film was shot in September, and Ruth and I had a hectic fortnight, travelling around to various sites where she could watch the performance. A derelict cottage at Gunheath, near Roche, was used as a replica of my home as it had been fifty years earlier. My christening ceremony was acted at Trethosa chapel, and I sat in a pew while a borrowed baby took my name. When this was over, Ruth moved about and chatted with the cast and crew. I was left for half-an-hour in the care of a ten-year-old St Austell girl called Zoe, who had a minor part in the film. She managed me very efficiently, and I was elated by the sheer novelty of the situation. I was soon writing more hilarious verse, stimulated by the three children who brightened the screen version of my wretched youth. I was struck by the contrast between these blithe pieces and the intense, mixed-up poems produced by my association with schoolgirls in the 1940s. Marriage had given me a new perspective: having Ruth to inspire my love poems, I found that other feminine inspiration stirred healthy humour or expressions of normal faith.

One incident which concerned my own appearance in the film was significant. Norman Stone was a persuasive young producer, but he could not induce me to be photographed writing or typing one of my old grim clay poems. I insisted that the camera must show me busy on a new poem entitled "Weymouth", pointing to the Promised Land, not back to the Egypt or the wilderness tortures which Rob Duncan was presenting.

At the end of March 1980 a group of us, including the three girls, went to London for the private showing of the film. The long train journey was enlivened by romps, but basic issues of destiny awaited us in the capital. Norman was acquainted with the current tenant of 50 Wimpole Street, and he had arranged for me and Ruth to be admitted to the premises. The original Barrett house had been demolished in the 1930s, but some features had been preserved in the flat which replaced it. I climbed the front steps that Browning had mounted in 1845 and fingered the marble moulding of the fireplace which Elizabeth Barrett must have touched.

Ruth and I were awed at being there at the source of the vision which had drawn me away from the despairing bachelor fate that brooded so stormily over the adolescent period of my life depicted on television screens. It was another delightful irony that a drama–documentary about my tragic background should open the door to this massive symbol of divine comedy. Our presence in the literal Wimpole Street was a bonus blessing, a seal and confirmation we had done nothing to bring about. Providence was being playful, and as we stepped out under the grey London sky I wondered what kind of happy trick God would perform next. The contrast with our visit to Hardy's birthplace appealed to the poet in me, the sense of design. Browning and Hardy represented the antitheses of my experience, and it certainly seemed that the cruel President of the Immortals had long been ousted by the benevolent Magician.

In *Ferishtah's Fancies* Browning said he could only speak from his "appointed patch" of sunshine: "All outside is past conjecture." He has been accused of bourgeois complacency and smug self-satisfaction—a charge that could never be made against me, as I spent nearly half my life in working-class poverty. But a Christian must witness to the rewards of his faith, giving proof that he has backed a winner, even if it was a hard preliminary process of self-surrender that forced him into his apparent good luck.

A strong antidote to complacency was soon administered as a direct result of Norman Stone's film, which was seen by millions on Good Friday. Among the Dorset people who were moved by it were the poets, David Boadella and his wife, Elsa Corbluth. Their eighteen-year-old daughter Eilidh had recently been burnt to death while training for Christian service in a Mother Teresa hostel in London. During the spring Ruth and I met David accidentally at a religious function, and he told us that his wife would welcome a visit from the man whose misfortunes had touched her so deeply. Maurice Gabb took us several times to the Boadellas' home at Abbotsbury, and on one occasion we stayed until after midnight, trying to give Elsa the comfort of faith. She was an agnostic, and I felt a heartrending poignancy as she allowed me to handle Eilidh's Bible and one of her coats. I stood silently at her grave, aware of a profound mystery, but not fearing that Eilidh's experience belied my creed. The yielding of one's life to Christ is a pledge of eternal triumph, whether one dies at eighteen or eighty. Some sort of martyrdom is inevitable in discipleship, which may mean a prolonged buffeting from adverse circumstances, as in my case, or a mortification of the ego in relatively trivial matters; for a few it is spectacular and from the temporal standpoint appalling. I knew that Eilidh and I shared the same pattern, and it was the Browning pattern:

"The evil is null, is nought, is silence implying sound;
  What was good shall be good, with, for evil, so much
    good more."

Eilidh had written a fair amount of verse since she left school, including poems which expressed her joy after conversion. The best of this work was collected and published in a booklet called *I Won't Paint Any Tears*, and I felt greatly honoured when I was asked to write an introduction to the poems. Though immature, they showed genuine talent.

In July we went to London again, travelling up from Weymouth for a showing of Norman's film at the headquarters of the Arts Centre Group, of which I was an honorary member. A thunderstorm raged while we were there, but I enjoyed answering questions from students and renewing my contact with Nigel Goodwin and Steve Turner, who had visited Goonamarris in 1977 to discuss the proposed film. We returned to Weymouth the same day, and throughout the rest of the summer I developed my Dorset friendships—chiefly with Evangelicals at Weymouth Baptist church. Each Sunday morning service there was now followed by frolics in the lobby as the Gabb children grew more confident about me. When we came back to Goonamarris that year the children came too, curious to see the strange claywork cottage from which their father had fetched us for four years in succession. Naomi's vivacious teasing added to the juvenile glow which had been brought into the house by the three child actresses.

Towards the end of the year an official envelope was delivered to our home one morning. I opened it and passed the letter to Ruth. A minute later she grabbed my hand and I could sense the startled dismay in her fingertip as she scribbled on my palm:

"They want to make you a doctor!" The letter was from Harry Kay, Vice-Chancellor of Exeter University, and it announced a decision to confer an honorary D.Litt. degree on me.

My first impulse was to decline the offer as totally incongruous. If such a suggestion had been made in my thirties I would have rejected it with a grunt of derision. I was the picturesque proletarian misfit, the uneducated Bunyan defying twentieth-century culture. But now in maturity I had come to see that such proud independence reflects a perverse egoism, that grunts of derision at kindly and well-considered gestures are not Christian. I therefore accepted the award, and Ruth, after the initial shock, was also pleased about it, anxious only regarding the correct dress she would wear for the occasion.

I thought it very appropriate when, in mid-July of 1981, the taxi that was taking us to Exeter University had to pick us up at Weymouth, not Goonamarris. The Cornish base was fading out. Most of the poems I had written since 1977 had Dorset subjects. I saw no future in Cornwall for my church fellowship or my youthful relaxation. There were rumours that Trethosa chapel would soon close. Cerris had left Portholland and was living in Devon. I met the St Austell girls, Zoe and her sister Kate, only two or three times a year when their mother brought them to our home for an hour. I often told Ruth it was time we settled in Weymouth and she usually agreed, though her deep friendship with Gwen Pearce, and the fact that my cousins and foster-sisters were accessible only in Cornwall, made her hesitate.

Pat Moyer and Cerris welcomed us at Exeter University, and I was soon introduced to Dr Kay. Just before the ceremony I was robed and given a wide-brimmed shallow hat. Ruth led me in the procession of graduands into the Great Hall, and sat with me on the platform. I was not at all tense or embarrassed there among the dons. I let some hymns run through my mind during the speeches. After Dr Kay handed me my diploma there was prolonged and vigorous clapping from the large assembly of students, then came the delicious luncheon and some playful minutes with Cerris. Later I was taken to the research library where many of my manuscripts were preserved. We arrived back in Weymouth tired but exhilarated.

The remainder of that year was uneventful for us at Goonamarris. We were still somewhat daunted by the practical difficulties of moving. My presence was occasionally requested at Cornish literary functions. In April 1982 Pat Moyer read my non-personal abstract mystical poem "The Winds" at a poetry recital given in the Roman Catholic church at Truro, organised to mark the publication of Charles Causley's religious anthology, *The Sun, Dancing*. Causley and I were on the platform with the priest, who was very friendly to me and Ruth and had paid us a visit. Ruth and I were sturdy Nonconformists, but we were touched by the new charitable spirit of the Catholic Church, and on the whole we responded sympathetically to Pope John-Paul's campaign in Britain during the next two months.

Our summer stay in Weymouth was unclouded, with many paddles on the Sandsfoot beaches, car and bus rides to the homes of friends, and a healthy blend of worship and fun at church and at the Aggie Weston naval fellowship centre on Portland, where we attended a Bible study every Tuesday and to which we sometimes went for Sunday afternoon tea. A Scottish naval officer, Hugh Steele, felt a close affinity with us and took us to various Christian gatherings. In the Rodwell house a phone-call from Norman Stone one evening startled us. He said he was bringing Sally Magnusson to the clay district in August to research a book she had decided to write about the Clemo romance and its background—a sharp contrast to her first volume, which dealt with the Evangelical athlete, Eric Liddell.

We returned to Goonamarris earlier than usual in order to give Sally the maximum help. We liked her forthright, warm-hearted personality from the outset, and soon she was squatting on our lounge floor amid a pile of papers, photograph albums and press-cuttings books. She tape-recorded Ruth's talk and I typed some information for her. Norman arranged a trip to Charlestown beach, inviting the St Austell girls also, and I had a hectic hour or two with Zoe on the sands. The situation was rather confused, as Sally wanted a weird, craggy clay area setting for her book. But I knew where the call was strongest, and I had already taken several boxes of books and files to the Rodwell house and left them there. The following summer Sally came to Weymouth for a week, and Ruth tried to explain why the palms now meant more to me than the clay-tips. Sally's book, *Clemo: A Love Story*, when at last it was finished after some initial difficulties, showed a remarkable insight into the transition process, the spiritual and emotional maturity that made a Weymouth home pin-point the drama of my theology.

Other shiftings and shapings marked the summer of 1983. It was the last time that any of the Gabb children came to Ruth's birthday party in July: only the two younger ones, Naomi and Jonathan, were present. I spent four happy hours with them, blackberrying on the cliffs and dancing around our back garden with Naomi. She was nearly thirteen then, a slim and attractive blonde, and I wondered whether this friendship, too, would soon fizzle out because of my inability to engage in the intelligent discussion which teenagers demand. We also had a visit from John Hughes, who had published books about the animals at his RSPCA centre near Taunton. He had recently married an old friend of ours called Sylvia and they brought her niece with them—a girl about Naomi's age. She was very gentle and reserved, though she sat with me on the settee and I wrote playful verses about her.

But she did not come to see us again, and Ruth and I had to face the problem of the childless elderly couple. We needed someone who would be permanently like a granddaughter to us. After prayer we decided that the best course was to advertise in a Christian journal for a foster grandchild, and Ruth did this in December 1983. There was a response from the mother of five-year-old Catherine Labdon. Catherine's father would soon be ordained as a vicar in Liverpool, and the parents proposed to bring her down to Cornwall at Easter. She arrived one Sunday afternoon—a pretty golden-haired little girl, very shy but sweet and winsome. During that week the Labdons took us to Gorran, Newquay and Polperro. Ruth had serious talks with them, and although there was to be no legal transaction it was made clear that we were to take the place of Catherine's real grandparents, who were dead. When she returned home we began sending her letters and presents, and occasionally a long-distance phone call would be put through, in which Catherine chattered with increasing freedom to "Granny".

We also got a response from Vicki Horton, a cultured Midlands woman whose daughter Lucy was already eleven years old. We had not considered taking on two foster grandchildren, but we accepted Lucy as a young friend. She and her parents visited us, and I started and kept up a lively correspondence with her.

Whether these developments helped to spur us into action about our Weymouth move I cannot say. We were becoming exasperated by our own indecision, and one evening in September I dropped into the Rodwell pillar-box a letter informing our landlords that we were ending our tenancy of the cottage in October. About tea-time on the 18th of October James Morgan reached Goonamarris with a hired furniture van and took my desk, bookcase and old typewriter, and the ancient farm dresser, to the Morgan-Moyers' holiday home at Portholland. Next morning, with the assistance of a neighbour, he loaded the rest of our furniture into the van, and in mid-afternoon we set off for Weymouth. I felt no wrench at leaving the cottage: it held too many bitter memories of hardship and frustration which not even my marriage could erase while I lived there.

The ensuing weeks were chaotic in the Rodwell house. Ruth and Bella struggled to find room for our furniture, empty the suitcases and boxes and fill drawers and cupboards. By the New Year things were tolerably in order, and I was soon encouraged by signs of fresh blessing on my work. In February 1985 I learnt that *The Invading Gospel* was being reprinted and that an up-to-date preface would be required. A few months later *The Shadowed Bed* was accepted—the allegorical novel I had written in 1948–50 under Brenda's inspiration, and with Brenda herself (called Bronwen in the story) as one of the chief characters. Ruth had not wanted this novel published during our residence in

Cornwall, since it portrays the clay district as the devil's territory. At the beginning of 1986 we gave approval to the manuscript of Sally Magnusson's biography. The publishers of my novel had urged her to finish it quickly so that it could be issued as a companion volume. While these two books were being prepared for publication my collection of poems, *A Different Drummer*, was accepted by a Cornish press, and by that time I could see the fruits of prayer in the area of friendship as well as in my literary field.

Naomi had been converted and had told us that she was to be baptised. Catherine had appeared in Weymouth twice and had lost her bewildered recoil from my handicaps. We were becoming much indebted to the Ramsdens, a Russian Orthodox family who lived at Totnes Priory in Devon. Father Benedict Ramsden had been a warm admirer of my work for many years, and had even gone to Goonamarris and Trethosa chapel in search of me after I had moved to Dorset. He had been given my Weymouth address and in August 1985 he brought his wife and three of his children to our home. During most of the visit his daughter Sophie was writing on my palm: she had heard her father speak of me so often that she was not at all nervous. Benedict had a mystical vein and he had sensed that although I had once known the "dark night of the soul" it was now as remote from me as measles.

He gave a talk on my books and presented me with an icon at Exeter University in March 1986 when a celebration of my seventieth birthday was organised there by Pat Moyer and Dr Ronald Tamplin. It was an informal event, almost a family gathering. Catherine had travelled all the way from Liverpool, with her parents, in order to show up at "Grandad's birthday party." Andrew Symons had arrived from Cornwall to expound my religion, Donald Rawe read one of my slapstick dialect tales, and Cerris recited a comic rhyme from *The Bouncing Hills*. Elsa Corbluth read some of my serious poems, and poetic tributes to me were offered by Paul Hyland and Harry Guest. Ruth and I were thrilled by this generous recognition, though not in an inflated worldly way. Ruth felt it as a vindication of her faith in

God and in her sense of a vocational marriage.

A different kind of thrill rewarded us in July when we attended Naomi's baptismal service. I had told her in a letter that I would have been baptised years ago if I were not so handicapped. I tried to share as far as possible her public profession of faith. She came to me soon after her immersion: I found that her hair was still wet, and before long I had mentioned the haunting spiritual beauty of those moments in one of my best Dorset poems, "Open Waters."

In August Ruth and I went with Catherine and her parents to Portholland and spent a refreshing week at the Morgan-Moyers' old home, which they now rented to their friends for holidays. It was a curious dwelling, formerly a Methodist chapel, standing in a remote rocky cove, only a few yards from the beach. Catherine took me for short walks and I enjoyed paddlng with her. Ruth guided me to our old Goonamarris furniture, which seemed weirdly isolated there so near to the sea, but I could not be drawn back. It was Ruth who was troubled by nostalgia, especially when Gwen Pearce drove over to the cove one day and took us to her Newquay home for a few hours.

Christmas came, and with it the first hint of the incredible climax that followed logically from our visit to Wimpole Street. Benedict and his wife had just returned from Venice, and while discussing the trip in our Rodwell lounge they asked if we would care to accompany them on their next flight to Italy. It was a startling proposal, but we could not decline it on the ground of expense. Poverty was now as far from me as bachelor quirks. (In the event, Benedict helped generously with the costs.) We liked the idea, and our Priory friends realised that to me such a visit would not be just a pleasant holiday abroad, but something relevant to my belief in *pattern*. We entered 1987 with images of gondolas and palaces shining in the background of our minds.

But the foreground was still Weymouth and would remain so after the Italian interlude was over. Benedict thought it best to defer the trip until autumn, but we did not simply sit down and wait. Our Dorset life was rich and varied even without Venetian splendour being added. In May we experienced a remarkable weekend. On the Friday Ruth's interview for the BBC *Woman's Hour* radio programme was broadcast—an honest and forthright testimony. Next day I achieved my first Dorset poetry reading, an hour's recital of my poems being given by Pat Moyer and Elsa Corbluth at Dorchester County Library to an audience as large as any I had drawn in Cornwall. Benedict was there, a striking figure with his beard and Russian-style dark robe. Sophie sat with me throughout the performance. On the Sunday Norman Stone's film about my youth was shown at Weymouth Baptist church, and the congregation was deeply moved. Some women wept as they embraced Ruth. I answered religious questions and then stood for a while with Naomi and her friend Sharon. Her elder brother Paul, who led the young people's Praise music group, came across to congratulate me. I always felt spiritually exhilarated among teenage Evangelicals: they were such a radiant contrast to the sick and shallow permissiveness of the godless majority of their generation. They were the only adolescents to whom God could make the Biblical promise which had been so abundantly fulfilled in my own life: "Ye shall eat in plenty and be satisfied, and praise the name of the Lord your God, that hath dealt wondrously with you." (Joel 2:26).

Immediately after this eventful weekend we relaxed with the Labdons at Torquay for a few days. We toured Paignton zoo with Catherine, sharing her delight in the monkeys and elephants and nearly suffocating in the heat of the jungle room where there were snakes I was glad I couldn't see. On another day Catherine and I faced the indignity of being put in the stocks at Cockington and viewed by passers-by as condemned criminals. In the summer the Horton family came down to Weymouth and stayed a week in a caravan near Sandsfoot Gardens. I had plenty of fun with teenage Lucy, her friend Karen and the little dog Welly.

The day of our great adventure arrived at last, late in October. The whole party—eight of us altogether, including Bella and Benedict's children—travelled to Heathrow airport and spent a night there in a hotel. Next morning after the tedious business of having our luggage ransacked, we boarded an Italian plane, and about noon I felt the strange new sensation of being lifted smoothly into the sky. Ruth sat close to me, both of us being loosely strapped. We enjoyed every minute of the two hours' flight across Europe. I wished I could see the weird panorama of landscape and seascape that fascinated my companions: soaring above the Alps was especially impressive, the snowy peaks looking, Ruth told me, no bigger than Cornish clay-tips. The young Ramsdens—Sophie, Emma and teenage Simeon—sometimes chattered excitedly and were sometimes mute with wonder at glimpsing the perspective of astronauts. We landed at Venice airport and were taken by water-taxi to our hotel in St Marks' Basin. The spell of this unique city had soon gripped me without actual sights and sounds. After our unpacking in the Italian bedroom we walked to St Mark's Cathedral for an evening service and knelt among devout Catholics.

The following day brought the peak we had anticipated. It was the 26th of October, the nineteenth anniversary of our wedding, which made the Browning link particularly apt. In mid-morning we were carried up the Grand Canal on a vibrating water-bus, and alighted near the massive Palazzo Rezzonico. A long flight of steps led up to the ornate entrance. Benedict showed officials a letter of introduction supplied by Exeter University, authorising me to be admitted to the Browning shrine, and soon we were inside, mounting and descending stairs, leaning over balconies, and finally standing in the fairly small room where Browning died. I felt as awed as at Wimpole Street, but no sadder, for I too had "never doubted clouds would break," and I endorsed the poet's farewell message: "Greet the unseen with a cheer!" Ruth shared my reaction, and we stepped quietly out into the chill air that eddied up from the canal.

A little later we found our way to a floating station, and after waiting amid a jabber of Italian from alighting passengers we lowered ourselves into a gently rocking gondola for the honeymoon trip I had promised Ruth. There was a curious romantic rhythm in the movement of the craft as the gondolier began dipping his oar in traditional style. Ruth pressed closer to me, sometimes holding my hand or playfully poking me to make me feel how inevitable this enchanted odyssey was. We passed under many bridges, including the famous Bridge of Sighs, and Ruth got splendid views of most of the city. We circled around through the narrower canals and the smaller blocks of islands. It was all soft and dreamlike, aglow with history, linking us with the days when Doges had sailed here to drop wedding rings into the Adriatic. Our focal point was nearer, in the gondola excursions the Brownings must have enjoyed during holidays while Elizabeth was alive. And now, with the hypnotic glide of the old-world craft, amid the palaces and churches, undimmed by the sunless sky, I could affirm the lines of my poem "Emigrant" which had been published a few months earlier:

"There's blue sky above every warm road
That leads to my feasts: no fight for a foothold!
I believe, no longer darkly,
Despite God's silence and frown, but because
The whisper came and the smile spread
Till, much surprised, I am awed by His pampering."